Interview
With an
Exorcist

AN INSIDER'S LOOK AT THE DEVIL, DEMONIC POSSESSION,
AND THE PATH TO DELIVERANCE

FR. JOSÉ ANTONIO FORTEA

FOREWORD BY MOST REVEREND SAMUEL J. AQUILA,
BISHOP OF FARGO

ASCENSION

West Chester, Pennsylvania

Ascension
Post Office Box 1990
West Chester, PA 19380
1-800-376-0520
ascensionpress.com

Cover design: Devin Schadt

Printed in the United States of America
21 22 23 24 25 12 11 10 9 8

ISBN 978-1-932645-96-5

Contents

St. Michael Prayer

Saint Michael the Archangel,
defend us in battle.
Be our protection against the
wickedness and snares of the devil.
May God rebuke him, we humbly pray;
and do thou, O Prince of the Heavenly Host,
by the divine power of God,
cast into hell, Satan and all the evil spirits,
who roam throughout the world,
seeking the ruin of souls.

Amen.

Foreword

We live in a skeptical age, one which finds the very idea of personified evil spirits to be a superstitious remnant of the Middle Ages. Those people—and religious traditions—who believe in the existence of the devil and demons are often ridiculed as being out of touch with modern times. The contemporary Western mentality is that evil is merely the result of an inadequate social environment or due to purely psychological factors, causes which can be remedied with a social program or medication. In this view, the only "exorcisms" necessary are those which rid our society of poor social conditions, ignorance, or psychopathology. Many Christians—among them not a few Catholics—have succumbed to this mentality as well. They are formed more by the culture in which we live than by the Gospel of Jesus Christ and the teaching of the Church.

Yet even a cursory reading of the gospels gives us many explicit references to the reality of demons and demonic possession. Indeed, we can see that deliverance from evil spirits played a central role in Jesus' ministry, and Jesus Himself cited these healing acts as proof that He was the Messiah (Mt 12:28; Mk 3:22-27). Our Lord cast out demons by "the finger of God" (Lk 11:20), by His own divine authority. Jesus commanded the demons to depart and they obeyed (Mt 8:16; Mk 9:24). The ministry of Jesus was essentially one of reconciliation and healing, the salvation of souls. Throughout the gospels, we see Jesus healing people's physical and spiritual illnesses, and among these people were those possessed by evil spirits. Exorcism of evil spirits clearly was an act of healing.

This same ministry of exorcism and healing Jesus handed on to His apostles, granting them the authority to cast out demons in His name from the very beginning of their ministry (Mt 10:1, 10:8; Mk 6:7; Lk 9:1, 10:17). Furthermore, when the apostles asked Jesus to teach them how to pray, He gave them the powerful words of the Our Father, including its concluding line, "deliver us from evil." As the *Catechism of the Catholic Church* explains, these words do not merely refer to some abstract notion of evil or sin; they refer to evil personified in malevolent spirits, particularly in Satan, "the Evil One" (see CCC 2851-2854). While this petition generally refers to the devil's ordinary temptations, it also encompasses the notion of demonic possession and oppression.

When needed, the Church continues to exercise this ministry of Jesus, carefully discerning when true possession is present and permitting those priests who have been trained in the rite of exorcism and with the permission of their bishop to perform it. In the cases of oppression by evil spirits or curses, a renouncement of the evil spirit or a breaking of the curse through the Sacrament of Penance and the deliverance prayer brings about healing.

In this fascinating, easy-to-read book, *Interview with an Exorcist: An Insider's Look at the Devil, Demonic Possession, and the Path to Deliverance*, exorcist Fr. José Antonio Fortea brings to light crucial aspects of this important ministry. He addresses 110 practical questions about the devil, demonic possession, and the path to deliverance. In the process, he provides bishops, priests, and laity alike with sound guidelines for determining the influence of evil spirits and the important spiritual questions it raises. Catholics need to learn to recognize the reality of evil, evil spirits, and the Evil One. In this way they may learn to discern in the spiritual life between good and evil, between the Truth—Jesus Christ—and the Father of Lies—Satan.

I do, however, have an important warning for you. Although all Catholics should have a basic understanding of the reality of evil, we should also avoid being overly preoccupied with the topic of the devil. The Evil One is capable of using such a fascination as a means to ensnare us—with despair, fear, or discouragement. We need not fear! "There is no fear in love, but perfect love casts out fear" (1 Jn 4:18). In the call to holiness—intimacy with the three divine Persons of the Trinity—we are encouraged to keep our focus always on the love that Jesus Christ has for us.

As the author of Hebrews reminds us, "Lay aside every weight, and sin which clings so closely, and let us run with perseverance the race that is set before us, looking to Jesus the pioneer and perfecter of our faith" (Heb 12:1-2). Jesus' deepest desire for all people is that they come to know the love of the Father for them and live in the heart of the Trinity. St. Ignatius of Loyola calls upon us to know Satan as "the enemy of human nature." He asks us to pray and to discover places in our hearts where we hold on to unbelief or are weak in faith. It is here that the Father of Lies will tell us that we are not the beloved of the Father of Jesus, our Abba. Indeed, if we attend humbly to receiving the love of the Father where we sense the depth of our human frailty and powerlessness, we can taste anew St. Paul's experience of God's healing love and power making us strong (see 2 Cor 12:9-10; Heb 11:34).

Additionally, when tempted, we should not despair or become discouraged, for Jesus has experienced the very same (Heb 4:15). Jesus Christ has won the victory over sin, evil, and death through His passion, death, and resurrection. By His grace, we can recognize and reject Satan and his empty promises. The Lord in His tender mercy will unbind any shackles of evil and sin we bring to Him! I pray that as you read this book you will come to know the freedom that Jesus Christ desires for you and has bestowed on you. May all of us "with confidence draw near to the throne of grace, that we may receive mercy and find grace to help in time of need" (Heb 4:16).

—Most Reverend Samuel J. Aquila, D.D.
Bishop of Fargo

Introduction

I have chosen to write this book in a style based loosely on that of an ancient scholastic tract—that is to say, a work composed of a series of questions of similar length and different theological weight—while at the same time reading like a modern interview. I have always been fascinated by those old scholastic volumes, written in ornate gothic lettering, in which theological topics were considered according to the interests of the particular monk or religious and dictated to a secretary. Why? Well, because it seems to me the freest and most interesting manner in which to deal with important theological topics for the non-academic reader. In short, I felt it necessary to treat this somewhat difficult subject in a way that takes into account all the crucial aspects and details—which is most critical to any discussion of demons and demonic possession, given the dangers that lie in an erroneous understanding—while still making the matter as accessible as possible to the ordinary reader.

Thus, *Interview with an Exorcist*, unlike the university thesis I previously wrote on the topic of exorcism, is not plagued with footnotes and erudite quotations, i.e., the kinds of things that academics consider so important. The questions and answers are organized in a logical sequence and according to general categories, but not in some highly formal structure. As I indicated, I sought to write a freer, more popular work, one that would appeal to a larger, non-scholarly audience.

The reader will notice that, in addition to referencing official Church sources (e.g., the Bible and the *Catechism of the Catholic Church*) and the wisdom of the saints, I refer in many answers to my own experiences as an exorcist. Several exorcists have reviewed the manuscript and have confirmed that these experiences mirror their own.

In the end, it is hoped that the questions that follow are answered in a way that truly enlightens you on this often neglected but vital topic without, of course, engendering an unhealthy curiosity in such matters. We need always to remember that Jesus has already triumphed over Satan and sin in His passion, death, and resurrection (see CCC 1708).

I. ANGELS AND DEMONS

1. What is a demon?

A demon is a spiritual being of an angelic nature that has been condemned for eternity due to his rebellion against God. As pure spirits, demons are not made up of matter. Because they do not have bodies, demons are not inclined to any "sins of the flesh" (i.e., it is impossible for them to commit the sins of lust or gluttony). The sins of demons are exclusively spiritual. But they can tempt human beings to sin in matters of the flesh.

Demons were not created evil. (In fact, it is impossible for God, who is Goodness itself, to create anything evil.) Remember: demons are just "bad angels." After God created the angels, He tested their fidelity to Him before admitting them to the Beatific Vision, the sight of His very essence. For purely spiritual beings, this "seeing" of God's essence would be a purely intellectual vision. Some angels obeyed the divine test; others did not. Those who disobeyed were irreversibly transformed into demons and cast out of heaven.

It may seem surprising that some angels would choose to hate God. But we need to understand that those who rebelled saw God no longer as a good—as *the* Good—but as the oppressor of their freedom. Hate was born as their wills resisted the call of God and held fast to the decision to leave the Father's house.

> Now war arose in heaven, Michael and his angels
> fighting against the dragon; and the dragon and
> his angels fought, but they were defeated and there
> was no longer any place for them in heaven. And
> the great dragon was thrown down, that ancient
> serpent, who is called the Devil and Satan, the
> deceiver of the whole world—he was thrown down
> to the earth, and his angels were thrown down with
> him (Rv 12:7-9).

How can purely spiritual beings fight among themselves?
What weapons do they use? Angels are spirits, so their
battles must be purely intellectual. The only weapons
that they can use are intellectual arguments. The angels
gave reasons to the rebels for why they should return
to obedience to God. The rebel angels countered with
their reasons to support their position and spread their
rebellion among the faithful angels. In this epic angelic
battle, some who were inclined to rebel returned to
obedience, while some of the faithful angels were seduced
by the evil arguments of the rebels.

In art, demons are depicted as deformed and grotesque
beings. This would seem appropriate given that demons
have definitively decided on a destiny far from God. The
interior loneliness in which they find themselves forever
and their envy of the faithful who enjoy the Beatific Vision
continually bring them face-to-face with their sins. They
hate God, themselves, and all those who seek to serve God.

But not all suffer the same pains. Some angels were
deformed more than others in the battle. Those who were
more deformed suffer more; the least deformed suffer
less. The intellects of the rebellious angels were deformed

and darkened by the very reasons they used to justify the rebellion of their wills against God.

Their plight is similar to the moral debasement that humans can suffer through sin. We need to remember that we are composite creatures made up of soul and body. Aside from the sins that are proper to the body, the internal psychological process that leads a good person to end up in the Mafia or as a guard in a concentration camp or a terrorist is essentially the same as the sequence of acts of intellect and will that led to the fall of the bad angels.

Though we are body-soul composites, we as humans have only to look into our own interior life to understand how we can fall into sin. In this light, the sin of the angels becomes more easily understood.

2.   Are all demons the same?

No. We have already seen that each demon sinned in a certain way and with a determined intensity. While the angelic rebellion against God had its roots in pride, from this root other sins grew. This can be clearly seen during an exorcism, when the particular demons possessing the person display sins of anger, self-worship, and desperation, among others. Each demon has its own psychology and its own way of being. For example, some are talkative, others are mocking; some are proud, others are hateful. Even though they all turned away from God, some demons are more evil than others.

As St. Paul and the tradition of the Church indicate, we need to remember that there are nine hierarchies of angels (from highest to lowest): seraphim, cherubim, thrones, dominions, virtues, powers, principalities, archangels, and angels. The superior hierarchies are more powerful, beautiful, and intelligent than the inferior ones. According to St. Thomas Aquinas, each angel is completely different from other angels. In sociological terms, there are no angelic "races"; rather, each one is its own species. As we have said, though, it is possible to group the angels into hierarchies. These hierarchies are also called *choirs,* since these groups form themselves into choirs that sing praises to God. Their praise is obviously not that of the voice, but rather a spiritual type of praise that comes from their will to know and love the Trinity.

Because some angels from each of the nine hierarchies sinned and transformed themselves into demons, a demonic hierarchy exists. In other words, there are demons that are principalities, virtues, powers, etc. Even though they are demons, they retain their particular angelic power and intelligence.

Exorcisms have shown that superior demons can have power over inferior ones. What does this power consist of? This is something that is impossible for us to know because we cannot see how one demon forces another to do something, since there is no body to push or force. Nevertheless, a more powerful demon can prevent a less powerful one from leaving the body of a possessed person during an exorcism. Even though the weaker demon is suffering and wants to leave, the stronger one may impede it.

3.   **Do demons experience time?**

Yes, in a sense. As pure spirits, angels and demons exist

outside of earthly, material time. However, they do experience a type of "spiritual" time—"a before and an after" to their acts of understanding and will. Whenever we speak of "before" and "after," we are speaking of some sort of time. This time is called *aeveternal* (from the Latin *aevum*), a succession of acts of understanding and will in a spiritual being. (St. Thomas Aquinas in the thirteenth century speaks about *aevum* in the *Summa Theologica*, I, 10, 5.)

Therefore, when we say that the spirits in heaven and hell are in "eternity," we need to understand this as an unending temporal succession (i.e., the passing of time without end) from a distinct beginning (i.e., the moment of their creation). Strictly speaking, only God is eternal; only He has "no time." God experiences past, present, and future as eternally present.

4. **What is the difference between the natural, preternatural, and supernatural?**

The *natural* deals with the laws of the physical world, i.e., the workings of nature, whereas the *preternatural* concerns things or events which appear outside or apart from (Latin *praeter*) the laws of the physical world. The *supernatural* concerns things or events beyond or above (Latin *super*) any created nature; it is proper only to God Himself.

Demons can engage in preternatural activities such as making an object levitate or transforming something instantly. They can do things that go beyond the material world, but they cannot act beyond their angelic nature. Their powers are limited, even in the physical world. God can create something from nothing; a demon cannot.

We can see these realms operating in our souls. For example, beautiful scenery can remind us of the beauty of God, and this is something natural. Meanwhile, an angel or a demon can send inspirations directly into one's mind. God can go further than that—He can send spiritual graces (of repentance, of thanksgiving, etc.) to the deepest depths of one's spirit, causing radical changes in a second. All working of grace is supernatural; grace is always sent directly by God.

5.   What do demons do with their time?

In the world of demons, like that of people, some do one thing and others do different things. Demons, of course, cannot build houses, grow food, construct machines, nor do any of the things human beings spend so much time on. Most of the time, demons occupy themselves with going deeper into the world of knowledge, in having relationships among themselves, and in tempting people.

The intellectual world is such a vast world that the demons occupy themselves in it completely like us. In a university, for example, there can be hundreds of professors with each one specializing in some branch of knowledge. Hundreds of professors and deans work hours daily in a university and all this work and activity produces just one thing: *knowledge*. The same thing happens in the world of the angelic spirits.

Relationships among pure spirits may not seem important, but the demons have real, complex social relationships. These relationships are not based merely on knowledge but also on the pleasure of communicating with one another and helping each other tempt humans.

6. **Is the devil merely a symbol of evil, or does he really exist?**

Demons are personal spiritual beings, as is the chief demon, the devil. Those Christians who deny the existence of demons and say that they are merely symbols of evil are heretics. Against this false belief stand the teachings of Christ, the teachings of the Bible, and the teachings of the Church (see *CCC* 391–395).

7. **Why did God put the demons to the test?**

The real question is, Why did God not grant all the angels the Beatific Vision from the first moment of their creation? Why did He take the chance that some of them would rebel against Him and become demons? God could have created angelic spirits and immediately given them the grace of the Beatific Vision. This was perfectly possible for His omnipotence, and it would have been perfectly just to do so. But there were some powerful reasons for testing the angels before granting them the Beatific Vision.

First, God had to give to each rational being a degree of happiness. Everyone in heaven sees God, but no one can enjoy Him to an infinite degree; this is impossible for a finite being. Each finite creature enjoys to the fullest degree possible without wanting more. A common analogy used to understand this metaphysical concept is that of a glass: God fills each glass (i.e., soul) to the rim but each glass is a specific size based on its degree of glory.

God, in His wisdom, decided that each angel would determine its degree of glory for eternity by its response to a divine test. Each angel determined its degree of happiness by the degree of generosity, love, constancy, and other virtues it displayed in the test. A spirit can grow in its faith and in its generosity toward God *before* it sees Him. But once admitted to the Beatific Vision, no further growth is possible—there can no longer be growth in faith where there is vision. Above all, the period of testing offered the angels the opportunity to grow in the theological virtues, and some angels would grow more in the virtue of perseverance, others in humility, others in petition, etc.

Offering a being the possibility of faith also supposes the risk that in this same being evil may flourish instead of faith. God, by giving free will to the angels and human beings, knew that freedom, once bestowed, could be used for good or evil. Of course, God could have created the cosmos in any way he liked, without any restrictions or limits. But a saint is not created; one becomes a saint through the action of grace. The gift of freedom allows for a Hitler as well as a Blessed Teresa of Calcutta (Mother Teresa). Once the gift of freedom has been given, consequences—good or evil—flow from every act of the will. In the material cosmos there is no spiritual good; the good of the cosmos is purely physical. Spiritual (or moral) good is qualitatively superior but necessarily requires a free choice. Thus, the appearance of moral evil in no way upset God's plan. The possibility of evil was already part of the divine plan before the creation of thinking beings.

Finally, the most important and powerful reason for God's granting angels the gift of freedom was for them to love. God loves His creation, and He desires to be loved in return. But love requires receptivity—it must be received freely (CCC 1828). The same God who can create the cosmos with only an act of His will cannot create that love that is born and proven in the suffering of the faith. The love of God is not created; it must be freely given by a created being.

8. **What does a demon think about?**

Every demon retains the intelligence of its angelic nature. Demons know and inquire with their minds about the material and spiritual worlds, the real and conceptual worlds. As spiritual beings, demons are eminently intellectual; there is no doubt that they are deeply interested in conceptual questions. They know very well that philosophy is the most elevated of the sciences and that theology is built upon philosophy. In spite of this knowledge, every demon hates God.

Though demons find pleasure in knowing, they also suffer as a result of their knowledge—especially when this knowledge leads them to think about God. Demons constantly perceive the order and beauty of the Creator in all created things. Even in apparently neutral things, they see the reflection of the divine attributes.

Demons are not constantly engaged in tempting human beings. Much of the time they spend thinking. They suffer during those moments when they remember God and become conscious of their miserable state, that is, their separation from God. As we have previously noted, the amount of this suffering varies in intensity according to each demon's degree of moral deformation.

9.   What language do the demons speak?

Demons, as pure spirits, do not need a language to communicate with each other; they simply communicate at will through the power of thought. Human beings communicate through words, which are symbolic representations of our thoughts. Spiritual beings, on the other hand, transmit thought in a pure state without the need for mediation or signs.

10.   Where are the demons?

Demons—like the souls of deceased human beings—do not occupy space. This does not mean, though, that they are in some other physical dimension. What does being or not being in a dimension mean for a spirit? They are not *anywhere*. They exist, but they are not "here" or "there" in a physical sense.

A demon is said to be *in* a place when it *acts* in that place. If a demon is tempting someone "here," one says that it is "here." If a demon possesses a person's body, we say it is present within the person. If a demon causes a chair to move, we say that he is *in* that concrete place. In all these cases, though, the demon is simply *acting* there.

Heaven, hell, and purgatory exist now only as states of being. At the resurrection at the Last Judgment, the souls of the dead will be reunited with their bodies and will then exist in a concrete place (see *CCC* 650, 1005). At that point, the blessed will occupy a "physical heaven" (that is, a physical place of everlasting happiness), and the condemned will occupy a "physical hell." As Revelation 21:1 states, "Then I saw a new heaven and a new earth."

After the general judgment, then, the blessed—souls reunited with their resurrected bodies—will dwell in the "new heaven and a new earth" for eternity. Where will condemned humans dwell? We do not know for sure. Some have speculated that the "physical hell" of the damned will exist in the center of this same world.

11. Do demons know the future?

No. Demons do not have knowledge of future events. In addition, what belongs to human freedom is undetermined; they do not know in advance our free choices. However, since their intelligence is far superior to ours, they can often *predict* the future simply by observation and deduction. With their superior intelligence, they can see the effects of certain causes whereas we would perceive nothing. Thus, there are times when they can accurately predict what will happen, even though the most intelligent of human beings would not even suspect such a result, no matter how many factors are analyzed in the present. On other occasions, due to the complexities and variability of human action, even the most powerful angelic intellect can be mistaken in its predictions.

12. Can a demon perform a good act?

We need to remember that demons are not engaged in doing evil 100 percent of the time. Sometimes, they just think. Doing this is not evil at all; it is merely an act of their nature. Nevertheless, demons cannot perform a supernaturally moral act (for example, an act of charity, supernatural repentance, or sincere glorification of God) because such an act requires supernatural grace.

A demon will glorify God only if it is forced to. It may regret having gone away from God, but without any true repentance or sincere pleas for forgiveness. As such, a demon can do many other natural acts with its intelligence and will. But a demon will never have the least amount of compassion or love toward anyone. This is impossible as a result of its rebellion against God, who is Love itself. A demon's heart only hates; it revels in the suffering of others. By their own free choice, the demons will feel an acute absence of the life-giving presence of God's love for all eternity.

13.   Do demons experience pleasure?

Yes, but only in a spiritual sense. As a pure spirit, a demon can derive pleasure only with his intelligence and will. Intellectual pleasures might seem less intense or real than the pleasures of the senses, but this is not the case. Pleasures of the intellect can be as sublime and varied as those of the five senses. Think about the enjoyment that reading a good book, playing a game of chess, or attending the symphony brings; such pleasures are eminently "spiritual"—that is, intellectual—even though the senses may be involved.

In spite of the demons' drifting far from God, their spiritual powers—intellect and will—remain intact. So their ability to experience pleasure remains intact as well. What they cannot do is love someone with a supernatural love. The capacity to love has been annihilated in the psychology of a demon. A demon knows but does not love. The pleasure achieved in doing an evil act is the same as that which a human being feels when he gets revenge on an enemy—it is a pleasure filled with hate.

14. Who are the most evil of all the demons?

One might logically assume that the most perverse demons would be those of the highest angelic choirs, but this is not the case. There is no relation between nature and sin. A demon of the lowest choir can be much more perverse than a superior demon. The evil that a free being can commit does not depend on the intelligence or the power that one possesses. An angel of the lowest hierarchy could exercise its virtues more than one of the more exalted hierarchies. In the same way, a humble, uneducated woman who devotes her entire life to doing God's will can be holier than an archbishop or a pope.

Here's an interesting related question: Is the hierarchy of angels the Bible gives us (angels, archangels, principalities, etc.) a hierarchy of grace or of nature? In other words, are the seraphim the holiest of the angels or merely the most powerful? Do they simply shine with a greater glow of angelic intelligence? It would seem that the angelic hierarchy is one of nature rather than holiness, since the visual description of the four living beings around the Lamb (the angels of the highest hierarchy) gives an impression of more power and knowledge, as do the very names of the nine hierarchies. *Principalities* and *powers* are names that seem to indicate strength more than anything else.

15. Does God hate the demons?

No. God, being perfect, is Love itself. The created world is God's act of love, and as part of His creation, demons remain *essentially* good and loved by God. It is true, though, that God "hates" sin because it harms the perfection of His creation. Sin ultimately leads to the condemnation of those who remain unrepentant, but this does not mean God hates sinners.

This is the terrible thing: The condemned cannot ask mercy from God because they have made a definitive choice. Infinite Love acknowledges this choice made in freedom. In *The Divine Comedy*, Dante places the following inscription on the entrance to hell:

> Through me is the way into the woeful city;
> through me is the way into eternal woe;
> through me is the way among the lost people.
> Justice moved my lofty maker: the
> divine Power, the supreme Wisdom and the
> primal Love made me. Before me were
> no things created, unless eternal, and I
> eternal last. Leave every hope, ye who enter!

This inscription, though a work of literature, captures the truth that it is *Love*, not hate, which allows the existence of hell. Thus, one cannot plead with Love to destroy hell. God loves the demons but condemns them nevertheless. Why? Because they have *chosen* hell by their rebellion against Him—God is simply ratifying their choice.

As an aside, if God does not hate the demons, an exorcist cannot hate them, either. During an exorcism, a demon may say things to try and incite hatred in the exorcist or others who are present. I recall an exorcism in which a mother lost control, becoming furious and enraged with the demon that possessed her daughter. The demon, with all the calmness in the world, smiled evilly and said, "You can't get rid of me with hate." In the end, only the power of love defeats evil.

II. THE REALITY OF EVIL

16. What is evil?

Evil is the lack (or privation) of a good that should be present in a thing. For example, blindness is a physical evil because it is the absence of the ability to see, which is proper to a human being. In moral terms, sin is the absence of a particular virtue in a person. As such, evil is not something that exists in itself; it is merely the absence of the good (see CCC 309, 314).

This classical definition, formulated by St. Thomas Aquinas in the thirteenth century, was the result of centuries of thought and the refinement of complex formulas into this simple, objective explanation.

17. Does evil really exist?

Yes, it does. The first thing we need to know is that evil—like good—is an objective reality. Though many in today's culture insist that morality is merely one's personal opinion and is subjective ("what's right for you might be wrong for me" and vice versa), this is a very grave error. Who could successfully argue that such things as illness, murder, abortion, torture, hate, poverty, and war, are not true, objective evils? Even those who are the most enthusiastic defenders of the subjectivity of good and evil find their position uncertain when confronted by such a monstrous evil as the Holocaust. When we see the film clips of the Nazi concentration camps, we can understand that evil exists apart from all cultural values and conditioning, apart from our own opinion of it. We can see that the reasons why someone might commit these crimes do not matter, nor does it matter what percentage of the population supports such actions. Certain actions are always objectively evil, regardless of our opinion about them.

18. Will evil exist forever?

Yes, in a certain sense. The clear teachings of Sacred Scripture and the Church affirm that both demons and condemned human beings will exist for all eternity in hell. In this sense evil will exist indefinitely. Evil will exist forever within these fallen angels and humans. At the end of time, the divine order will be established in a perfect way; God's truth will triumph. But those beings that have consciously chosen to reject God and serve evil will be separated from him and burn eternally in the fires of hell.

19. What are the types of evil?

While the variety of particular evils is infinite, theologians typically distinguish between *physical* and *moral* evils. Remember our earlier definition of evil: the lack (or privation) of a good that should exist in a thing. Here's a good example of a physical evil: the painting the *Mona Lisa* is good, but a knife mark left by a vandal would be an evil because it causes a lack of something that should be present, i.e., the integrity of the painting. Water is good, but a lack of water—a drought—produces dehydration, starvation, forest fires, etc. Everything that exists is essentially good, even though it may have defects, because it was created by God who is all-good.

When a person knowingly chooses to act against the law of God, he commits a moral evil, a sin. While physical evils cause much suffering, moral evil is more heinous because it flows from the free choice of men (see CCC 310–314 for a detailed treatment of the nature and types of evil).

20. Does "infinite evil" exist?

No, evil is limited. Evil always exists in a finite being; it does not exist in itself. While an infinite being (i.e., God) can exist, infinite evil cannot because it is merely a lack (or privation) of a good that should be present in a being.

But, one may ask, couldn't an infinite being deform itself infinitely? Here's the problem: to degrade itself, this infinite being would have to desire something disordered. Having all the fullness of being in itself, it cannot desire anything outside of itself. As such, the possibility of an infinite lack (i.e., evil) in an infinite being is logically and metaphysically impossible.

Thus, temptation is impossible for God. He cannot sin since nothing can attract Him to evil. God cannot desire anything outside of Himself.

21. What is the greatest evil?

According to the *Catechism of the Catholic Church*, the greatest evil is sin (CCC 1488). Since God is love and sin leads to the rejection of His love, sin inevitably leads to hatred—of God, of humanity, of those around us, and of ourselves. Those who allow themselves to walk the path of hatred can reach the point where they hate all four objects with their entire strength. Such a consuming hate is the final stage of total moral degradation.

III. Demonic Activity

22. Should we be afraid of the devil?

The devil strives to do all the evil that he can, especially by tempting us to turn away from God through sin. If he could do more evil, he would. If a person prays the Rosary daily and asks God to protect him from all the snares of the Evil One, he has nothing to fear. The power of God is infinite; that of the devil is not.

God, through His gift of sanctifying grace, has given us a powerful weapon against Satan. St. Paul tells us: "Put on the whole armor of God, that you may be able to stand against the wiles of the devil" (Eph 6:11). The words of St. John are equally encouraging: "We know that any one born of God does not sin, but He who was born of God keeps him, and the Evil One does not touch him" (1 Jn 5:18). And Jesus Himself assures us: "Behold, I have given you authority to tread upon serpents and scorpions, and over all the power of the enemy; and nothing shall hurt you" (Lk 10:19). The words of Jesus are categorical: nothing can harm us if we are in Him.

For a Christian, fear of the devil is completely unjustified, for faith in God casts out all fear. As a child, St. Thérèse of Lisieux had a wonderful dream which she relates in her autobiography:

One night I dreamed that I went out for a walk alone in the garden. Arriving at the stairs that had to be climbed so as to get to the garden, I was frozen to the spot with fright. In front of me, near the bower, there was a barrel of lime and on the barrel two horrible looking little devils were dancing with surprising agility given they had irons attached to their feet. Suddenly, their inflamed eyes looked towards me and then instantly, showing themselves to be much more scared than I, they jumped off the barrel and went to hide themselves in the clothes room that was there in front. Seeing that they were not very brave, I wanted to see what they were going to do, and so I approached the window. The poor little devils were there, running over the tables not knowing how to hide from my sight. Sometimes they came close to the window looking with suspicion to see if I was still there; and upon seeing me they began to run desperately around the place again.

Certainly this dream has nothing of the extraordinary. But I believe nevertheless that God allowed this dream to be remembered always, to show me that a soul in the state of grace has nothing to fear from demons, who are cowards capable of running away from the look of a child. (*Story of a Soul*, chapter 1)

Similarly, St. Teresa of Avila, in her *Autobiography*, writes:

Seeing, then, this Lord (God) is so powerful as I see and know He is, and that the demons are His slaves—of which there can be no doubt, because it is of faith—and I am a servant of this Lord and King, what harm can they do unto me? Why have

I not strength enough to fight against all hell? I took up the cross in my hand, and I changed in a moment into another person in a short time and it seemed as if God had really given me the courage enough not to be afraid of encountering all of them. It seemed to me that with the cross I could easily defeat them altogether. So I cried out, come on all of you; I am the servant of our Lord. I should like to see what you can do against me.

And certainly they seemed to be afraid of me for I was left in peace: I feared them so little, that the terrors which until now oppressed me, quitted me altogether; and though I saw them occasionally, I shall speak of this by and by, I was never again afraid of them; on the contrary, they seemed to be afraid of me. I found myself endowed with an authority over them, given me by the Lord of all, so that I cared no more for them than for flies. They seem to be such cowards; for their strength fails them at the sight of any one who despises them.

These enemies have not the courage to assail any of those whom they see ready to give in to them, or when God permits them to do so, for the greater good of His servants, whom they may tempt and torment. May it please His Majesty that we fear Him whom we ought to fear, and understand that one venial sin can do us more harm than all hell together; for that is so. The evil spirits keep us in terror just because we want to.

... It is a great pity. But if, for the love of God, we hated all this and embraced the cross and set about

His service in earnest, [the devil] flees away before such realities as from the plague. He is the friend of lies, and the lie himself. He will have no pact with those who walk in the truth.

... I do not understand those terrors which make us cry out, Demon, Demon! When we may say God, God! And make Satan tremble. Do we not know that he cannot stir without the permission of God? What does it mean? I am really much more afraid of those people who have so great a fear of the devil, than I am of the devil himself. He can do me no harm. (*Autobiography*, chapter 25, no. 19-22)

Pope Benedict XVI, as Cardinal Ratzinger, wrote on the following on this topic:

The mystery of iniquity is so inserted in the fundamental Christian perspective, that is to say, in the perspective of the Resurrection of Jesus Christ and his victory over the power of evil. From this view, the freedom of the Christian and the sure trust that rejects fear (1 John 4:18) takes all its dimensions: truth excludes fear and as such allows the power of the evil one to be seen. (Quoted in *Renovation and the Power of Darkness* by Joseph Cardinal Suenens)

As you can see, our faith teaches us that the devil exists, but he exists in the theological construction of faith in God our Lord. Faith in God is incompatible with fear; rather, faith destroys all fear. As 1 John 4:18 tells us, "There is no fear in love, but perfect love casts out fear."

23. Can a person make a pact with the devil?

Many think that pacts with the devil only exist in literature, but they are mistaken. There are those who consciously, with full awareness and intentionality, make a pact with the devil and devote their souls to him in order to get something in this life. The notion of a formal pact with the devil appears for the first time in the fifth century in the writings of St. Jerome. This Father of the Church tells of a young man who went to a wizard so as to obtain the favors of a beautiful woman. As pay for his services, the wizard forced the young man to renounce in writing his faith in Christ. In the sixth century, we also see this type of pact in the legend of Theofilus, who agrees to be a servant of the devil and signs a formal pact. This legend was widespread in Europe during the Middle Ages.

Of course, one can write out a pact with the devil, but he is not going to appear. This is often discouraging to the person making the pact because he or she expects this to happen. Even so, if one invokes the devil for a particular purpose, it may come to pass (as in spiritualism, for example). On this topic, we also need to make the following points:

1. Making a pact with the devil does not mean that you will obtain a life of wealth, luxury, or fame. I personally know of two people who made such a pact, and to put it frankly, their material lifestyle is worse than mine. Neither does it appear that the devil was especially generous to them in a carnal way. We need to remember that the devil is a

deceiver; he is not God—he cannot give whatever he wants (see *CCC* 395).

2. A person can always repent of the pact whenever he wants to with a simple act of the will. Upon repenting, the pact they made remains as ink on paper, no matter what the terms of the deal were. Even if the possibility of repentance was excluded in the pact, such a clause is useless. God has given us the freedom to do as we want; we cannot renounce this gift. This is also valid in eternity—in heaven we will no longer want to sin and in hell we will no longer want to be forgiven, but our freedom remains intact.

Many seem to think that the devil can grant one success in business or in a profession, that he can give one wealth or fame. But, as we have said, the power of the devil is limited. Worldly success depends on a complex interplay of causes and effects. The devil can only tempt humans to be part of his plan—for example, he can tempt a manager to choose one worker instead of another. But this temptation can be overcome, so not even a simple thing like this is certain by making a pact with the devil.

The great destructive power of a demonic pact is that the person may think he is condemned no matter what he does. It is difficult for him to see that he is still as free as before to repent and revoke the pact he has made, returning wholeheartedly to God.

24. Can a demon cause a mental illness in a person?

Demons can tempt us, and they sometimes do so in a continuous way with great intensity. As such, a demon could provoke an obsession, phobia, depression, or another type of mental illness in a person. This can seriously disturb a person's ordinary life to the point of making him unbalanced. So, yes, a demon can cause mental illness—but only if God permits it. (Of course, everything that occurs must either be willed or at least permitted by God.)

Given the internal mechanism that is used to cause temptation—that is, the infusion of a thought or image in our intellect, memory, or imagination—this *modus operandi* can be used in such a pernicious way that it can unbalance a person. This is well within the power of a demon. The only thing that can prevent this activity is the will of God. So does God *always* prevent demons from causing a mental illness in a person? Undoubtedly, no. But this is the exception, not the rule. In most cases, mental illnesses have purely natural causes.

25. Can a demon cause a physical illness?

First, we need to clearly understand that physical illnesses nearly always have *natural* causes. The belief that sickness has its cause in the demonic world is rooted in a pre-scientific, superstitious worldview in which myth is substituted for reason. This being said, if demons exist, then the *possibility* exists that they may sometimes act to cause illness, but this is an extraordinary occurrence—i.e., it is outside the normal laws of nature. Normally only rain, snow, or hail fall from the sky, but meteorites also fall on rare occasions. It is the same case here; sometimes strange events happen.

St. Thérèse of Lisieux includes a very interesting chapter in her autobiography:

> The illness which overtook me came, certainly, from the demon; furious because of your entry into the Carmel [i.e., of her sister], he was determined to take revenge on me due to all the damage that our family would cause him in the future, but he almost made me not to suffer; I went on with my schoolwork, and nobody was worried about me. It was towards the end of that year that I was attacked by a continual headache ... This lasted until the Easter of 1883 ... it was while I was undressing that I had a strange fit of trembling ... I wish I could describe this strange illness of mine. I'm fully persuaded now, that it was the work of the devil ... I was delirious nearly all the time and talking utter nonsense ... often I seemed to be in a dead faint, without making the slightest movement ... it seems to me that the demon had been given power over the outward part of me, but couldn't reach neither my soul, nor my spirit, except by inspiring me very great fears of certain things. (*Story of a Soul*, chapter 3)

In an extraordinary and unusual way, God can allow a demon to cause a physical illness in a human being. In fact, St. Luke expressly mentions such a case: "And there was a woman who had had a spirit of infirmity for eighteen years; she was bent over and could not fully straighten herself" (Lk 13:11). The gospel text does not explicitly say that this woman was possessed but that a "spirit of infirmity" (i.e., a demon) was the cause of her sickness. To this we can add the sickness of Job and the death of Sarah's spouses caused by the demon Asmodeus in the book of Tobit, as well as the torments of such modern saints as St. John Vianney, the Curé of Ars.

26. How can one tell if a vision is demonic in origin or is a psychiatric problem?

The best way to discern if something is demonic in origin or merely a psychiatric problem is through the passage of time. If something that seems extraordinary (e.g., a vision or a locution) is a mental illness, it will get progressively worse and obvious psychosis will develop. When a person meets with his spiritual director or a theologian to discuss an extraordinary phenomenon he has experienced, it is initially very difficult—if not impossible—to discern what is actually taking place. After some months, though, the most obscure cases are clarified, and it becomes possible to separate a demonic influence from a mental illness.

For example, an unknown penitent kneels in the confessional and tells the confessor that the Blessed Virgin has audibly told him that she loves him and that he should be good. The priest has no way of knowing if the person has received a genuine locution or is suffering from a hallucination. Not even the greatest theologian in the world could know. But if the person confesses this phenomenon over time (e.g., a year or even less), the matter would become clearer. If the penitent is sick, his illness will gradually progress and he will say that the Blessed Virgin is revealing more and more things to him. Within five years, his mental instability will be obvious, not only to the confessor but also to his family and friends, due to the absurd and illogical character of his hallucinations.

As mental pathologies advance, they move further and further away from the laws of logic.

27. Can demons cause nightmares?

Yes, even though there is no way of knowing when a nightmare has a natural cause or a demonic one. We can only suspect that it has a demonic cause when there are other indications that point to this. There are cases where no psychiatrist has been able to find a reasonable explanation, either conscious or subconscious, for a normal person to suffer every night for a month or more with terrible nightmares that cause him or her to awake screaming and covered in sweat. These periods of very intense nightmares are sometimes connected to things such as having taken part in an occult rite or having begun a more intense spiritual life. The best advice one can give someone in this situation is to use holy water and ask God for protection and deliverance from any demonic influence during the night before he goes to sleep. If such actions cause the nightmares to stop, this would confirm that they were demonic in origin.

28. Can demons read our thoughts?

No. Though demons can tempt us, they cannot read our thoughts. With their great intelligence, they can *guess* what we are thinking—but they can never be absolutely certain. As spiritual beings, they are much more intelligent than we are, and as such, they can deduce things with greater accuracy and with fewer external signs than we can. But we always have to remember that demons are outside our souls; only God can truly read the soul. This being said, if one directs his mind and will to a saint, an angel, or a demon, they can hear us. So it does not matter whether our prayer is verbal or merely mental. In certain cases of possession I have observed that the demon obeys orders that have been given mentally.

29. Can demons cause disasters and accidents?

If demons had the freedom to cause natural disasters, the whole world would fall into chaos. So the short answer is no—demons cannot cause disasters and accidents at will. Why? Simply because God prevents them from doing so.

Storms, hurricanes, earthquakes, and other disasters ordinarily happen as a result of natural causes. Nonetheless, the book of Revelation does teach us that God, at the end of time, will allow a freer manifestation of the power of demons (see Rev 13:13-14), even to the point of affecting the physical world. But meanwhile we should not think that disasters or accidents have their cause in demonic action without strong objective evidence. Cases of *poltergeist* (the presence of a demon in a place evidenced by noises and the movement of objects) are proof that a demon can suspend something in the air or move an object. Since demons hate human beings and want them to suffer, it seems likely that if they were not restrained by God from causing continuous accidents, they would do so.

Once, I was praying for a lady who suffered from a demonic influence. Soon it began to rain, then hail, and the hail became gradually more intense. Then a strong storm wind began to buffet the church. The wind was so loud that I had to stop praying; no one could hear the prayers over the noise. We needed to shout to be heard.

The entire church creaked like a wooden boat in the ocean. Suddenly, the roof of the church gave out and lifted off in one of the corners. We prayed that the whole roof would not come off. It was an unforgettable scene: the wind furiously shaking the altar cloths (which did not blow away), the bricks falling on the presbytery from the highest part of the roof, and the thunder roaring without interruption.

Here we have an episode in which it is reasonable to think that there was a relation between the prayer upon that person and what happened afterward. A curious aspect of this event is that the nearest weather station did not detect any abnormal winds, so the insurance company at first refused to pay to repair the damage!

30.　What is the difference between magic and religion?

When we speak here of *magic* we are not referring to the popular art of the "magician" who pulls a rabbit out of a hat or makes things (apparently) disappear. Such "magicians" are just entertainers—*illusionists*—who use various techniques to trick our eyes.

In this discussion, the word *magic* refers to occult practices performed by witches or sorcerers. Throughout history, in many cultures, magic and religion came to be mixed to one degree or another. Nonetheless, we can see there is a clear and precise difference between these two realities.

- Religion is obedience (to God); magic seeks power (over forces or beings).

- Religion requires faith and worship; magic seeks control (over forces or beings).

- Religion requires us to change our lives; magic wants to change others through manipulation.

While religion is defined by *adoration,* magic is defined by *dominion* or *control* over supernatural forces or entities. It does not matter whether these forces are good or evil; a witch or sorcerer seeks to harness their power. In magic, one is not dealing with the transcendent, since God by His very nature is omnipotent and therefore unable to be dominated. As such, one is dealing with powers that, no matter how powerful they may be, can be dominated by a technique.

On the contrary, in religion, the believer deals directly with God, the Holy One, and a relationship exists between God and us—much like a parent with his children—in which we submit to His will and obey His commands. This relationship sanctifies us and keeps our minds and hearts focused on heaven. Magic, on the other hand, in the words of the *Catechism of the Catholic Church,* is "gravely contrary to the virtue of religion" because it "attempts to tame occult powers, so as to place them at one's service and have a supernatural power over others" (CCC 2117). Witches and sorcerers seek power rather than holiness. In addition, magic requires no conversion or change in the one who practices it.

31. Can demons unite and concentrate their efforts to influence society?

The greatest power of the demons lies in tempting us to

sin. Since they communicate among themselves, demons certainly work together and concentrate their efforts to influence human society. They do this by collectively devising strategies and by putting them into action in a specific place. While they desire to tempt everyone to sin, they know very well that certain individuals have the ability to influence society as a whole because of their wealth, fame, or power. The communications media are a particularly powerful influence on today's society. As such, the demons especially target these elites.

In politics, demons are never neutral—they always analyze the situation and focus their energies on those political officials and candidates who will (wittingly or unwittingly) favor their goals. Undoubtedly, in the German election of 1932, the demons understood perfectly that their goals would be better served by tempting the German people to vote for a rather unknown, fringe candidate named Adolph Hitler. Does this mean that Hitler's rise to power can be attributed solely to demonic forces? No, human choice was involved; but demons were undoubtedly involved, too. Similarly, the Church Fathers, in their writings about Christian persecution by the state, often point out that such persecution is rooted in the instigation of demons on rulers and the population as a whole.

We must always remember that the devil is the Father of Lies, and he seeks to make evil appear good and good appear evil. At the heart of much evil is the rejection of human dignity; the demons want us to forget that we have been created in the image and likeness of God.

There is the famous vision of Pope Leo XIII in which he

saw the infernal spirits concentrated on Rome. This vision was the origin of the Prayer to St. Michael, which the Holy Father sent to the world's bishops in 1886 and asked the entire Church to recite. The work of the angels and the prayers of Christians can impede the plans of darkness. This is why prayer and sacrifice are so important; they are a bulwark against the powers of hell in this world and a source of abundant blessings.

Though we must do battle in this invisible struggle with spiritual powers, we should always remember that in the exercise of our free will we are the authors of our own destiny. The demons can only influence us to the extent that we let them. In the end, we do what we choose and are ultimately responsible for these choices. Not even the concerted effort of millions of demons can *force* us to do something we really don't want to do. When tempted, prayer is our greatest weapon, a weapon as powerful as the greatest army or wealth. The demons know the power of prayer and fear it.

32. Can the devil have a human child?

No. This is absolutely impossible for the simple reason that demons are spiritual beings. A spirit, by definition, has no body, and therefore cannot procreate with a human being.

So the popular notion—which turns up frequently in novels and movies—that the devil, at the end of time, will impregnate a woman who will give birth to his child, and that this child will grow up to be the Antichrist, is not only contrary to the clear teachings of the Bible and the Church but is metaphysically impossible.

Even though a demon may appear in a corporeal (i.e., bodily) manner, it remains a spirit; it only *appears* to have a body. This appearance remains something external to its being.

33. Is the devil the "beast" in the book of Revelation?

No. The book of Revelation clearly distinguishes between the three key figures who will arise in opposition to Christ and the Church at the end of time: the Antichrist, the beast, and the dragon (or serpent). Whereas the Antichrist is a man, the beast is a political power that brings war to the earth. It is the dragon who is identified with the devil. There is no ambiguity or confusion in Revelation between these three distinct realities (see Rv 12, 13).

34. Why does the Bible call the devil "the prince of this world"?

On some occasions, the Bible uses expressions in reference to the devil that seem excessive. Nevertheless, everything in the Scripture is perfectly measured. In the Church's official Latin translation of the Bible, God is called *Dominus* (Lord) and *Rex* (King). There is only one King and one Lord; these two terms are always reserved for God in the Bible, that is to say, there is only one holder of power and one holder of rights.

God is King; the devil is just the "prince of this world." The Latin word for "prince"—*princeps*—means "he who occupies the first place; the most important, the principal one." By giving him this title, the Bible wants to convey without a doubt that the devil is the most important demon in this world. Thus, the writings of the holy Church Fathers, following these words of Scripture, consider the devil to have been the most powerful and beautiful of all the angels before his rebellion against God.

35. Do God and the devil really talk among themselves as in the book of Job?

In the Scriptures, Satan speaks with God to throw in His face the sins that men commit. But this is not a real and authentic conversation. So do *true* conversations take place between God and the devil? The answer is no.

Even though both God and the devil are spiritual beings (and spiritual beings, due to their very nature, generally like to communicate among themselves), true conversations between them do not take place. This is because the devil has no interest in conversing with God, whom he hates with all his strength. Conversely, God has no interest in having a conversation with a being who continuously breathes hate against Him. God has His perfect dignity, and this is why He does not want to converse with one who only insults and blasphemes Him all the time. In short, God does not want to talk to the devil because, in reality, there is really nothing for them to talk about.

36. Why is the devil called "the Accuser"?

> For the accuser of our brethren has been thrown down, who accuses them day and night before our God. (Rv 12:10)

Every time we sin, Satan rejoices, and he never lets pass an opportunity for pointing out our offenses to God. In this sense, he "accuses" us before the Creator. Remember: when the devil wants to talk to God, he only has to direct himself to Him. God listens to everything the devil says to Him; He knows every thought that comes from a demon. This type of communication between God and Satan is reflected as much in the book of Job when they both speak as in the book of Zechariah (see Zech 3:1).

Satan's only purpose here is to remind God of the many times he triumphs over us, i.e., the many times he is successful in tempting us to sin. After the Last Judgment, sin will no longer be possible and, as such, the devil will not be able to accuse us of anything.

37. Why is it said that Leviathan had various heads?

In Psalm 74:14, we read: "You crushed the heads of Leviathan." If Leviathan is only one being, why is the plural "heads" used?

Just as the pope is the visible head of the Church, and each pope is an individual person, each in turn is head of the Church. Similarly, throughout history, there are persons who are the visible and manifest heads of the iniquity and power of Satan, infamous figures such as Antiochus Epiphanes, Nero, Diocletian, Napoleon, Hitler, Stalin, and Pol Pot. Though the Church has only one head at any given time, Leviathan (i.e., evil) can have various "heads" simultaneously. While the Church forms a mystical body (the mystical body of Christ), evil does not. Good is order and unity; evil is disorder and dispersion.

38. Is God's greatest creation Lucifer or the Blessed Virgin Mary?

Before this question can be answered, we have to

understand that *Lucifer* (which means "morning star") was the angelic name of that angel before he rebelled against God and became a demon. I say "angel" because, while most theologians consider Lucifer to be synonymous with Satan, some think that he is a demon distinct from Satan. We also take as a given that Lucifer was the highest angelic nature created by God. Having made these clarifications, we return to the question at hand.

Strictly speaking, the highest nature that God has created was that of the greatest of the angels—Lucifer. The Blessed Virgin Mary, though, *became* the loftiest creature through her sacrifice, her works, and the grace of God (see *CCC* 490–493). Her exaltation was not an act of *creation* but of *sanctification*. God made Lucifer magnificent in his nature and he corrupted himself; God made Mary humble in her nature (a human being and, as such, inferior to the angels) and she sanctified herself. We can see that a sort of "inverted parallel" exists between these two figures:

- Lucifer is the most perfect creature by *nature*; Mary, the most perfect creature by *grace*.

- Lucifer corrupted himself by *disobedience*; Mary sanctified herself by *obedience*.

- Lucifer wanted to be king, refusing to serve, and in the end became nothing; Mary wanted to be nothing, desiring to serve, and in the end was crowned Queen of heaven.

There is a parallelism even in their titles—the "Angelic Star of the Morning" (Lucifer) and the "Star of the Morning of the Redemption" (Mary):

- The first star, Lucifer, fell from the angelic firmament; the second star, Mary, was elevated.

- The first star, which was spirit, fell to the earth; the second star, which was human, ascended to heaven.

- Lucifer did not want to accept the Son of God made man; the Blessed Virgin Mary welcomed Him in her womb.

- Lucifer is a spiritual being who ended up making himself worse than a beast (without ever ceasing to be spiritual); Mary is a human being that ended up becoming better than an angel (without ceasing to be human).

Now there is only one "morning star"—Mary. Not only did the first morning star fall; the second morning star shines even brighter. Mary's radiance is much more beautiful and intense than Lucifer's ever was because she shines with the light of grace, not merely nature.

IV. TEMPTATION AND SIN

39. Why do we sin?

We sin because, due to the effects of original sin, our wills have been weakened, and we give in to temptation. When we are tempted, we must choose between two options: doing good or doing evil, committing a sin or living in virtue. In temptation, the will has to choose between two options; it knows that one option is good and the other evil but feels attracted to choose the bad.

Temptation is not a defect of the intellect. If we did not know that a particular action was sinful, we would be ignorant and not guilty—subjectively speaking—of committing sin. To sin, we must *know* that we are choosing evil.* There is no sin without a bad conscience. This is what makes sin so interesting from the intellectual point of view: Why do we choose an evil *knowing* that it is evil? This is a real mystery.

The simple answer (but one which does not fully explain the matter) is that we sin due to weakness. While this is true, it is also true that we are not so weak that we are unable to resist temptation. God gives us the grace to do what is right and to grow in virtue—if we choose to live in His grace and allow it to increase within us through obedience to His will, and through prayer and the sacraments. If we were not capable of resisting temptation, we would have no moral responsibility, i.e., there would be no sin because we would have no choice. Sin requires us to consciously *choose* to do wrong. Therefore, although we are weak, we can always resist. We cannot excuse ourselves by claiming ignorance of the intellect or weakness of the will. We do evil because we want to.

It could be said that we do evil for the good we get from it. But the intellect, on some level, knows that any good we derive from sin is a "poisoned apple"—it will taste good in our mouths, but it will be sour in our stomachs. For example, we may choose to drink alcohol excessively on a particular occasion because we want to "feel no pain" and want to "drown our sorrows." But this "good" holds a lot of bad within it. No matter how attractive the "good" of a particular sin appears to be, our conscience tells us: "Don't do it." To say that we do evil because it appears to be good is an explanation for why we sin, but sin and evil remain somewhat of a mystery. Perhaps the "poisoned apples" we often eat—despite knowing them to be poisoned—can never be explained completely in this life.

Note: Since evil often presents itself as something good, we need to have a well-formed conscience, i.e., one that is formed in accord with the teachings of the Church and right reason (see *CCC* 1783–1785).

40. How many of our temptations come from demons?

No one can say what percentage of our temptations comes from demons and what percentage comes from our own weakness. It is true that the devil can tempt us at our weakest point, i.e., with those sins he knows we are particularly vulnerable to committing. But it seems reasonable to think that the greater part of the temptations come from ourselves. We don't need any external force to tempt us. Freedom is enough so as to use it badly. It is enough to have to make a decision and to consciously make the wrong decision—deliberately, with no apologies, without being able to throw the blame on anybody else.

It is true that the devil tempted the first woman, but we could have sinned without the devil's temptation, too. Sin does not need the external temptation of a demon; our own freedom is enough to produce it.

41. Can we distinguish temptations that come from ourselves from those that come from the devil?

There is no way to distinguish temptations of demonic origin from those that come from within us. Demons tempt us by infusing thoughts in our minds. In other words, a demon introduces into our reason, memory, and imagination intellectual objects proper to our understanding that cannot be distinguished from our own thoughts, such as the image of a tree, a memory, or a word. But an angel can also produce such ideas and communicate them to our minds. This is why there is no way to distinguish what comes from us, an angel, a demon, or God directly.

People who are devoted to their spiritual life and pursue an intense life of prayer can recognize those temptations that appear with a fairly surprising intensity and persistence without any discernible reason. For example, if one is reading a book contrary to the faith, we would expect him to experience temptations against faith. But if such a temptation suddenly appears for no reason, lasts for weeks, and is particularly intense, this may be a sign that the temptation may be from a demon. Even then, however, we cannot be sure. As a general norm, we can say that temptations that are persistent and very intense can be suspected to come from a demon.

Priests sometimes counsel spiritual people who have thoughts of blaspheming God or of stepping on a crucifix. If these temptations are chronic, it is reasonable to think that they are the result of mental illness. But if their appearance is sudden, and the person seems to be of sound mind, then there is reason to suspect that such temptations come from a demonic source.

To psychiatrists, we should point out that while we understand the mechanisms of the subconscious, we also need to remember that demons exist. An obsessive temptation can clearly be seen as demonic when it disappears suddenly one day and never returns. The temptations of a demon are never chronic and, no matter how vehement they are, do not leave any lasting effect on the psyche of the person.

42. Can we be tempted beyond our strength to resist?

No. Though we are weak creatures, God cares for us as His children. As the Bible states, "God is faithful, and he will not let you be tempted beyond your strength, but with the temptation will also provide the way of escape, that you may be able to endure it" (1 Cor 10:13).

God permits us to be tempted to test our obedience and freely choose His will. In the Bible, just before His passion, Jesus said to St. Peter: "Simon, Simon, behold, Satan demanded to have you, that he might sift you like wheat" (Lk 22:31). "Demanded" implies that the temptation must be allowed by God. Not to affirm this doctrine would mean that we are in the hands of blind destiny, and anyone could be tempted with a power and intensity beyond his strength to resist. Therefore, the message is clear and comforting: God, as our Father, watches out so that none of His children are pressured beyond what they are capable of. We can see in this the wisdom of the old proverb: "God claims but sustains." He gives each the grace to be strong in the face of temptation and choose good instead of evil.

43. What can be done against temptation?

We must immediately resist it with the help of God's grace. A temptation is harmless if we resist and do not entertain it. From the moment we begin to dialogue with a particular temptation, though, considering the pros and cons of what it offers, our opposition to it begins to weaken, and it is far more difficult to resist succumbing to it.

Confessors often see some very devout penitents who are at times overwhelmed with temptations to commit grave sins. Such religious people cannot understand why these horrible thoughts come to them; they feel guilty and powerless to stop them. Given the nature of demonic temptation, the best remedy is to pray and to ignore the temptation as much as possible and do exactly the opposite of what is proposed. Falling into despair is of no help, but successfully resisting the temptation causes the demons to despair.

We need to remember that while a demon can introduce thoughts, images, or memories into our minds, he cannot control our wills. We can be tempted, but in the end we do what we *choose* to do. Not even all the powers of hell can force someone to commit even the smallest sin.

44. Do demons have a plan when tempting us?

Remember: a demon is a spiritual being that possesses a greater intelligence than ours. Therefore, in temptation, a demon tries to enter into a conversation with the person he is tempting. If the person being tempted resists and never considers the temptation for even a moment, then it is a one-sided conversation—the demon speaks but gets no answer; his words are ignored.

But a demon can be at our side for a very long time, analyzing us and coming to know our particular weaknesses. He will then seek to tempt us at our weakest point. A demon is extraordinarily pragmatic, and he knows that the probability of success a type of temptation will have. If a particular person is virtuous and is therefore unlikely to commit a mortal sin, a demon will tempt the person with a venial sin. If he knows that even this temptation may be unsuccessful, he will tempt the person with an imperfection. For example, tempting an ascetic with gluttony would be a waste of time, but getting such a person to fast excessively would much more likely be successful. And, if the demon has success in this area, he will then try to tempt the person to fast in a way that builds up his pride or is most damaging to his health.

In another case, a demon knows that tempting a nun

to neglect prayer would probably not be fruitful, but tempting her to pray excessively and thereby neglect her work has a higher likelihood of success. Or to convince her that she does not really need to obey her confessor since he is a man and is less spiritual than she. A demon never tempts blindly but always analyzes and attacks where he sees there is some possibility.

The examples given above are of temptations directed toward people of prayer and virtue. The man given over to vice (i.e., a person who habitually commits mortal sins), on the other hand, has little protection. Without the armor of God's grace, his spirit presents numerous flanks that are unguarded and exposed to temptation. His passions are easily incited by the action of the demons. This is why we pray in the Our Father for God to "deliver us from the Evil One." Even though we are free to resist temptation, we need to constantly ask for the Father's protection and deliverance. This is why the Lord has given each of us a guardian angel—to counter the evil inspirations of the devil with inspirations to goodness and virtue.

Temptation is incompatible with prayer. If one is tempted and prays, the temptation disappears. Prayer creates a barrier against temptation, since in prayer our intellects and wills are centered on God. Eventually, a demon cannot resist this and leaves us alone.

45. Why does God allow temptation?

If God does not want us to sin, why does He allow temptation at all? We have the answer in the verse that says, "Count it all joy, my brethren, when you meet various trials, for you know that the testing of your faith produces steadfastness" (Jas 1:2).

Without temptation, there would be no opportunity for us to grow in virtue every time we successfully resist the allure of sin and remain faithful to God's will. It is true that God could restrain the demons so that they would be unable to interfere in the history of humanity, but He allows their diabolical work so that it can be an occasion of virtue for us. In other words, we could say that God permits a certain amount of darkness in this world (temptation and sin) so that a purer and brighter light (virtue and salvation) can be gained. So God allows temptation because He knows that much good can come from it if we resist.

46. What is eternal death?

The human soul, as a spiritual reality, is immortal (see CCC 366). Like any spirit, it is not subject to decay or illness; it cannot grow old or wear out. No matter what sins people commit, their souls cannot die in a metaphysical sense. They will exist forever. *Where* they will exist forever—heaven or hell—is another matter.

When we use the expressions "mortal sin," "death of the soul," or "eternal death," we are speaking of the death of the soul's *supernatural* life, i.e., the life of God's sanctifying grace (see CCC 1861). As Christians, we are admitted to this life of grace in baptism, and we are strengthened in grace through the sacraments, particularly the Holy Eucharist and confession. Mortal sin destroys this supernatural life, but the soul continues to exist in its natural state. The intellect and the will, with all their natural powers, continue to work, but there is no life of grace remaining within the soul.

Thus, many people are "alive" only on a purely natural level, without the supernatural life of grace that God willingly offers them. Without God's grace, one cannot be admitted to the eternal life of heaven; such a soul "dies" eternally in hell.

47. What is the process that leads to eternal death?

As St. James teaches, "Each person is tempted when he is lured and enticed by his own desire. Then desire when it has conceived gives birth to sin; and sin when it is full-grown brings forth death" (Jas 1:14-15). With great insight, these two verses describe the process that leads to the death of grace in the soul. Sin is not produced by itself nor does it appear suddenly before us in such a way that we are not at fault. Rather there is a process, as James describes:

> 1. The passions tempt.
>
> 2. Sin is conceived.
>
> 3. Sin is born.
>
> 4. Sin reaches its maturity.
>
> 5. Sin gives birth to death.

Note the comparison of the growth of sin with that of a mother carrying a child in her womb. The apostle James uses the phrase "to give birth" because sin has a conception and gestation period. While a particular sin is committed at a specific moment, it is conceived beforehand in our passions. No immoral act appears without a process, a hidden process developing in the heart of the individual. This is why we need to cultivate a life of virtue to help us keep our sinful tendencies in check.

Just as the first sin one may commit is the result of a process, so too every sin that follows. This process leads to the death of the soul, which, if persisted in until bodily death, leads to eternal death in hell. Knowing this should lead us to value the supernatural action of the divine grace which vivifies the soul. If we commit ourselves to growing in the life of grace by loving God, obeying His commands, and striving to die to our self-will, we need not fear eternal death.

48. Can one be condemned for "little" sins?

No. Eternal condemnation is so horrendous, so terrible, that it is reserved for grave sins. Only one who dies in a state of mortal sin is condemned to hell. This being said, *every* sin, no matter how small, is a step toward greater sin; every sin, no matter how slight, is a step in the direction of condemnation. No one can say: I will only commit this small sin once and I will never do it again. Every sin weakens the will, and every fault darkens our understanding a little more. Great sins would not exist without small ones. In its essence, every deliberate sin is one step closer to the precipice, one step closer to eternal damnation.

Some people are under the impression that avoiding "little

sins" is just something bishops, priests, and consecrated religious need to be concerned with. These same people claim that laypeople do not need to watch out for venial sins because, after all, they live in the "real" world. This is a serious error. Though venial sins cannot directly cause us to lose our salvation in Christ, we need to avoid them nonetheless. Little sins weaken us and can lead us to commit great sins. Jesus calls every Christian to be holy, to "be perfect, as your heavenly Father is perfect" (Mt 5:48). There can be no room in our lives for deliberate venial sins.

49. Are only those who *want* to be condemned actually condemned?

No one really wants to be condemned. But some *choose* to be condemned because their sinful actions exclude them from the life of blessedness. In the same way, no one really wants to spend their lives on earth full of hatred and wishing evil on one's neighbor, but some choose to live this way, much to their own suffering. Consciously choosing evil through a life of mortal sin and stubbornly persevering in sin until death will result in one's condemnation. God certainly does not want anyone to be condemned; He loves us and sent Jesus so that "whoever believes in Him should not perish but have eternal life" (Jn 3:16). But believing in Jesus requires us to be faithful to His will. As Our Lord told His disciples, "If you love me, you will keep my commandments" (Jn 14:15).

50. Is God present even in hell?

Yes, God is present even in hell. There is no place (or

being) in which God is not present. God, the Creator of all things, maintains everything in existence and knows everything from all eternity. So demons are not freed from the presence of God even in hell. No matter how far a demon wants to draw away from God, he will always be condemned to be in the presence of God.

Even though God is in hell, the demons do not directly perceive His presence. On the contrary, they feel totally distanced from Him. God permits them to have this sensation so as not to torment them. Nevertheless, there is no place or being that can be outside the reach, sight, or power (i.e., the presence) of God.

51. Why does hell need to be eternal?

Repentance can be born only of grace. If God does not send grace to a spirit, making it understand the perpetrated evil, then there can be no supernatural repentance. Without grace, a demon can understand that it was a foolish decision to have rebelled, a decision that has caused it suffering. But true repentance is qualitatively different from just mere awareness. It is not simply an act of the understanding; rather, it is a gift from God so that we might bend our knees before Him and humbly ask for His forgiveness. Without this grace, one may feel pain for making a wrong decision, but true repentance is beyond him. Demons can admit that their choice led to suffering, but this does not stop them from hating God.

The eternity of hell, then, is not due to some arbitrary divine decision. Rather, its eternal duration is a necessary consequence of rebellion against God. It is they who have drifted far away from Him and do not want to return. Many Christians think that God is excessively severe in imposing an eternal condemnation on sinners, but He is just giving those who hate Him what they want—eternal separation from Him (see CCC 1033–1037).

Some people think: *Well, no matter how much I sin, I do not want to go to hell and be separated from God. I will always want to ask for forgiveness.* With this kind of reasoning, they calmly go on sinning. To these people we need to say that many who are condemned to hell never thought that they would be. If one continues to sin, this will lead to increasingly more serious sins and eventually one will end up being confirmed in sin, making repentance all the more difficult. We can see this in the lives of those who abuse drugs. In the beginning, they were normal people who started to use drugs socially and in moderation. When they saw the pathetic state of drug addicts, they asked themselves how such people could be so weak and let drugs take over their lives so completely. Soon, though, the social users begin to use more and more, and eventually their state becomes as bad as those they condemned. It is the same with sin: those condemned to hell believed that they would not pass certain limits, that they would keep their sin "under control." But, as we have said, sin breeds more and greater sin, leading one further down the path to destruction.

But what about the devil? If he repented right now, couldn't the devil do an intense penance for millions of years to be purified from his sins? This seems like a reasonable question since we know that there is no sin that cannot be forgiven. But the condemnation of the devil (and that of the other demons as well) is not primarily a problem of sin per se; it is a problem of the will. The devil's condemnation is eternal because his choice is, in the words of the *Catechism of the Catholic Church*, "irrevocable" and not due to a "defect in the infinite divine mercy" (*CCC* 393).

Thus, it is impossible for the devil to do penance and return to God. He (and the other demons) possessed the power of an angelic intellect. Unlike us, he did not suffer from a weakened will or a darkened intellect. He knew full well the consequences of his rebellion against the divine will.

It is the devil's own will that impedes his repentance, and it is certain that no demon or condemned soul has ever repented. Without grace, repentance is impossible. The condemned will not receive this grace since they have already made their definitive decision: *non serviam* ("I will not serve"). Thus, the circle has been closed around hell for all eternity.

52. Why does God not just annihilate the demons?

God, in His great love, has pledged not to destroy any intelligent being He has created. Demons, by their very existence, are a manifestation of God's justice, a proclamation that the law of God is not violated without consequence. He who violates this law deforms himself and, if he chooses not to repent of this transgression, his deformation becomes eternal. Such is the case with the demons. They are a terrifying proof of the divine order.

In a certain sense, even the demons enrich the perfect order of God's creation. Beauty cannot be destroyed by ugliness; rather, ugliness (i.e., evil) makes us see beauty all the more by contrast. A cathedral would not be more beautiful if we took away the monstrous gargoyles adorning it. As has been said, the demons show us the justice of God, His holiness and wisdom in creating such an order. While it would have been better had sin and evil never entered creation, their presence can point the way to what is good, true, beautiful, and holy. Even a majestic cathedral, with its high towers and sculptured beauty, has its gloomy crypts.

For the demons, the centuries pass with no hope. Undoubtedly, being desperate and full of sadness, if they could commit suicide, they would do so in order to end their suffering. But, as a pure spirit, the life of a demon is indestructible. A spirit has no organs, it cannot be poisoned, and it cannot be starved. It cannot even die of sadness. No matter what is done, it will continue to exist forever. (Of course, the same holds true for human beings as well. We will exist forever—either in heaven or hell, by our free choice to obey God or reject him.)

Anyway, as has been said, even though the demons suffer for all eternity, they do not suffer at each and every moment. Even though they do not recognize it, their existence is a gift from God. And even though they fall over and over again into acts of hate, reproach, and remorse, the rest of the time they know and experience a natural existence, which is proper to their nature.

53. Why does Sacred Scripture say that demons are in the "regions of the air"?

Put on the whole armor of God, that you may be able to stand against the wiles of the devil. For

we are not contending against flesh and blood,
but against the principalities, against the powers,
against the world rulers of this present darkness,
against the spiritual hosts of wickedness in the
[regions of the air] (Eph 6:11-12).

Sacred Scripture, when speaking of demons, always locates them in one of two places: in *hell* (that is to say, in "that which is below") or *in the air*. To say that they are in the air is a way of saying that they are everywhere, that they move about with complete freedom. St. Paul repeats this again when he calls the devil "the prince of the power of the air" (Eph 2:2).

When the Bible says that some demons are in hell, does this mean that they are not on earth tempting us? This is probably the case. What also seems to be the case is that there is no difference in suffering between those who are in hell and those who are tempting mankind.

54. When Jesus was on earth, did the demons know He was the Messiah?

As we have said, demons do not know everything. They do not even know all that happens in this world; they are among us, but they come and go. The demons watch over the saints in a very special way, and they knew that Jesus was a man who was especially holy. They could see that He had never committed a sin or even an imperfection. The devil, though steeped in sin, is the consummate appraiser of virtue. Though the demons could observe Jesus living a perfect life, His divinity is an invisible attribute. When Jesus began performing miracles, the demons would have discussed among themselves whether He was just another prophet or the Messiah. They would have increasingly begun to suspect that Jesus was the Messiah, not only because of what He did but also because of His teachings. While the apostles, in their weak moments, may have been inattentive to Jesus, the demons certainly heard and remembered every word He said.

It was clear that Jesus was not an ordinary man because He performed miracles that were beyond that of angelic nature (e.g., raising the dead). At first, though, the demons could argue that it was not Jesus who performed these miracles but God. They could not distinguish whether He did them by His own power; they only saw their effect. But it soon became clear to them—from all the biblical and theological signs, all the miracles, and Jesus' goodness—that this man was the incarnate God. This knowledge can be seen in the biblical stories of possessions when the demons ask, "What have you to do with us, O Son of God? Have you come here to torment us before the time?" (Mt 8:29). These words indicate that they knew Jesus was God, the same God who would condemn them at the Last Judgment.

55. What order do the three temptations of Jesus in the desert follow? Is there any significance to this order?

In the synoptic gospels, we see how the devil tempted Jesus in the wilderness immediately prior to the start of His public ministry (see Mt 4:1-11; Mk 1:9-15; Lk 4:1-13). These temptations were those of bread, power, and worldly recognition. Now then, why would the devil tempt Jesus to worship him when he did not even get Him to break His fast? In the end, why did he tempt Jesus with jumping off the pinnacle of the Temple? If Jesus had already rejected the glory of the whole world, why is the devil's last temptation seemingly so minor?

At first sight, it seems logical that the devil's temptations of Jesus would have started with the *greatest* sin, and not achieving this, the devil would have moved on to lesser sins. So he would first tempt Jesus with idolatry and follow up with something that is not even a venial sin, such as breaking a voluntary fast.

But one's first impression is that the succession of the devil's temptations does not follow a logical order. Actually, the succession of the devil's attack follows a more subtle logic. It follows the order of temptations that a soul suffers when it decides to move forward with living a spiritual life. That is why there is a deep symbolism in these three temptations. The devil first tempts Jesus with things of the flesh, symbolized by the bread. This temptation symbolizes what the ascetic calls the "night of the senses." If the soul resists this type of temptation (i.e., all the bodily appetites), there is no reason for the devil to continue tempting in this way because the soul has fortified itself against it. Having passed through the night of the senses, the devil then tempts with the world. The soul feels the beauty and attractions of the world that it has left. This is a symbol of the "night of the spirit." Here, the soul is tempted by the world in which it lives but no longer enjoys. If this temptation is resisted, one final danger remains: pride. This is pride in the gifts one has received from God.

These three temptations symbolize the phases of temptations we go through in the spiritual life. It has to be added that, concretely, those which the devil used with Jesus were especially subtle:

- First, the devil tempted Jesus not with sin per se but with imperfection. He was asked to stop doing a good, i.e., his fasting, and turn stones into bread.

- Then, He was tempted with the spiritual good of the world. It is as if the devil were saying, "Make a sign of acknowledgment toward me, proud as I am, and, as a reward, I will put myself at your side. All I ask is that you acknowledge me, and I will help you in your work of saving souls. Are you not humble? Are you not capable of lowering yourself a little more for the eternal good of souls?" This second temptation is packed with tremendous spiritual meaning. Jesus was not asked to stop being God; He was only asked to humble Himself a bit more. Could not the Just One, who had made so many sacrifices for souls, make one more? It is the temptation to do a little evil so as to achieve a great good.

- The final temptation is that of pride—to be publicly recognized. It was to prescind from the fact that it is God, in His time, who exalts His servants. Here, the devil was saying, "Even though God decides the time and the moment, why not bring the moment forward? Why remain in obscurity when so much good can be done by coming out into the light in a glorious and spectacular way?" We can see that this third temptation is the most complex and subtle of all.

56. Why does Satan appear more frequently in the New Testament than in the Old?

The term *Satan* appears eighteen times in the Old Testament and thirty-five in the New. *The devil* can be found thirty-six times. The term *demon* appears twenty-one times in the New Testament, while the Old Testament's equivalent terms for demon (Lilith, etc.) appear much less. The New Testament is shorter than the Old, yet the demons appear more frequently. Why is this?

I believe that this is because the Lord did not want to infuse fear into His chosen people. Also, He wanted to prevent false, dualistic beliefs about good and evil from taking root among them—i.e., the belief in a "god of good" and a "god of evil." That is why God gives the demons a lower profile in the Old Testament than in the New. God Himself is the central figure of the Old Testament, and the angelic world only appears on a certain number of occasions so as not to encourage idolatry. Nevertheless, in the New Testament, divine revelation is completed and the existence of this spiritual world is shown in a more profound way. With the coming of Jesus, the kingdom of God was at hand; He was reclaiming the world from slavery to sin and the temptations of the devil.

V. Demonic Oppression and Possession

57. Why doesn't Satan appear to humanity and show all his power?

There is no doubt that, if Satan showed himself openly under the appearance of an angel of light, many people would follow him. He could do signs and portents, cure illnesses, and predict the future. St. Paul tells us the reason why Satan does not deploy his faculties openly:

> And you know what is restraining him now so that he may be revealed in his time. For the mystery of lawlessness is already at work; only he who now restrains it will do so until he is out of the way. And then the lawless one will be revealed ... the coming of the lawless one by the activity of Satan will be with all power and with pretended signs and wonders (2 Thess 2:6-9).

Satan is proud. He wants to be worshiped, and since people are weak, many will be tricked. The one thing he cannot do is show his power because God restrains him from doing this. Though he hates God and tries to do all the evil he can, Satan is bound to the designs of God's will. And the will of God is that he not be able to show himself openly until the end of time. Until then, his manifestations are limited to those satanic groups to whom he shows himself when he is invoked. It is these extraordinary acts and the ordinary actions (temptations), and with the concentration of demonic forces in certain places and specific moments, that the "mystery of lawlessness" is already at work, though it has not yet been revealed. In the spiritual life, chaos and disorder always bear the seal of the Evil One.

58. Why does holy water disturb demons?

The real question is: How can something material have an influence on something spiritual? It would seem that these two realms are so distinct, so independent, that something material should not have any effect on a demon, much less expel him. Actually, though, a material object—holy water, holy chrism, etc.—can torment or expel demons because the Church has given a spiritual power to this object by blessing it. In other words, the Church, with the power she has received from Christ, can join a spiritual effect to an object. Of course, the object itself has no power; rather, the power lies in that of Christ Himself which has been placed upon the particular object.

In any event, in my experience there are materials that have a concrete effect because of what they symbolize. Here is an anecdote that touches on this fact: One winter day, extremely cold weather had frozen the pipes in my parish, and we had no water. A possessed girl I was exorcising could not be given water from the holy water fonts because it was several days old and many people had dipped their fingers in it. As I was preparing to go out in search of water, I remembered that there was a bottle of lemonade that had been left over from a meeting of catechists. It occurred to me to bless the contents of the bottle, thinking that the type of liquid was of little importance since its power was rooted in the prayer attached to it. I discovered, though, that its effect on the demon was much less than normal. After a few minutes, I ordered the demon in the name of Jesus to tell me why this was so. He resisted, but in the end he told me that, while any blessed liquid might have some effect on the demons, holy water is more effective because it symbolizes purity and cleanliness. (In fact, every material the Church blesses or consecrates—water, wine, bread, salt, incense, oil, etc.—has a deep and powerful symbolism.)

59. What other objects disturb demons?

A crucifix, even if it has not been blessed, is particularly powerful. It torments the demons because it reminds them of their defeat by Jesus' death on the Cross, of the final triumph of Christ over evil and death, and of their ultimate condemnation at the Last Judgment. Similarly, relics of the saints torment demons because they are filled with the spiritual anointing of these saints and call to mind the life of heroic sanctity the particular saint lived. The same is true for all religious images, whether they are blessed or not.

60. How can we protect ourselves from the attack of a demon?

As has been said, the best shield and armor against the attacks of the Evil One is prayer, the sacraments, good works, and living a spiritual life. Some people think specific—and repeated—prayers are needed for protection against the devil, but this is to think of prayer in "magical" terms. Strictly speaking, it is not a particular prayer that protects us but the action of God Himself. When we give alms or do works of mercy, it is the grace of God that fills us with spiritual light; it is sanctifying grace which moves God to shower His blessings upon us, thus making us an unpleasant dwelling for a demon.

Of course, before performing any work or facing a specific danger relating to the demonic field, the invocation of St. Michael the Archangel is highly effective. He always comes to our aid and protects us if we call on him with faith. Even though St. Michael has received a special charge from God with respect to demons, one can also call upon his or her own guardian angel, another saint, or God directly for protection. Fortunately, there are mothers and grandmothers who pray to God every day for the spiritual protection of their children and grandchildren. As the mission of the Mother of God is to pray for the whole Church, so the mission of these faithful women is to pray for their families.

Those who would like to protect themselves against demonic attacks should remember the words we proclaim during every Mass before receiving Holy Communion: "Lord, I am not worthy to receive you, but only say the word and my soul shall be healed." In the Holy Eucharist, Jesus enters into our bodily dwelling with His body, blood, soul, and divinity. Our body is like a home or tent in which He comes to dwell. Nothing destroys demonic influence more powerfully than worthy reception of the Body of Christ.

Remember: the devil is only a creature; his power is limited. In the end, he cannot prevent God's ultimate plan and purpose from being accomplished (see CCC 395). Under the wings of our guardian angel, under the cloak of our Blessed Mother, and with Jesus entering every day in our hearts, we should not fear the demon's attack.

61. Why do the demons use the bodily senses when they possess someone?

I do not have an answer to this question, so I will limit myself to making the following points. I have observed countless times that a demon is tortured by sacred things through the bodily senses of the possessed. A demon inside a person can sense when one approaches him with a crucifix, but it tortures him when placed on the body of the possessed. Why does holy water torture a demon when it is sprinkled on the person's body and not by being close to him? Why does the demon feel horror when one orders him to look at an image of the Blessed Virgin but does not feel this horror when the person's eyes are closed?

Severe bodily pain may cause the possessed to snap out of his trance state. Also, if his nose is stuffed up or some part of the body is itchy during the exorcism, I have observed that the person will blow his nose or scratch himself. It is as if the demon, while possessing the body, feels whatever the bodily senses feel at a given moment. Whatever upsets the body also upsets the demon. As an aside, we might point out that many spirits leave the body with an expiration through the mouth or nose.

It is clear that demons use the body of the person so as to feel things. But it is also interesting to note that they also use the body to express their feelings. During an exorcism, the demon will unwillingly show signs of pain, anger, or joy by shouting, crying, or smiling malevolently. For example, a demon may show sadness by causing the possessed to cry. He may not want to show himself, but by the end of the exorcism the demon finally shouts with horror such phrases as "I can't anymore" or "I'm off."

62. What is more important, confession or exorcism?

As human beings, we are dazzled by that which is the most spectacular to our eyes. Confession is not very spectacular; its work is very quiet and discreet. Nevertheless, confession is a divine gift much greater than exorcism. Exorcism only drives out a demon from one's body; confession drives out evil from one's soul. Confession destroys our attachments to iniquity and gives us sanctifying grace. Confession not only forgives but heals our soul and fills it with light. Frequent confession strengthens us with sanctifying grace and is a powerful force in helping us resist temptation (see *CCC* 1458).

63. Is it correct to insult the demons?

And the LORD said to Satan, "The LORD rebuke you, O Satan! The LORD who has chosen Jerusalem rebuke you! Is not this a brand plucked from the fire?" (Zech 3:2).

Yet in like manner these men in their dreamings defile the flesh, reject authority, and revile the glorious ones. But when the archangel Michael, contending with the devil, disputed about the body of Moses, he did not presume to pronounce

a reviling judgment upon him, but said, "The Lord
rebuke you" (Jude 1:8-9).

Bold and willful, they are not afraid to revile the
glorious ones, whereas angels, though greater in
might and power, do not pronounce a reviling
judgment upon them before the Lord (2 Pt 2:10-11).

The above Scripture texts from St. Jude and St. Peter
make reference to certain pagan cults in the early days
of Christianity that, among other things, insulted evil
spiritual beings during their rites. Maybe these insults
were directed towards *daemones* (genies) or, more probably,
eons, spiritual figures who appear in heretical Gnostic
teachings. Importantly, both apostles censured this
activity, pointing out that not even the angels insult the
demons. Though they rebelled against God, the demons
continue to possess a glorious nature, far superior to the
natures of the material cosmos. That is why the angels do
not insult them; they do not want to insult beings who,
like them, stand at the apex of God's creation.

These very interesting verses show us that just the angels'
asking God to restrain or rebuke the demons is enough to
torment them. Even the demons cannot resist the divine
power when God restrains the powers of their nature. It
is even worse when He rebukes them; the scolding of God
must be something terrible since the angels threaten the
demons with it.

The angels are in the presence of the Most High, and His
holiness is so great that they do not want to blemish their
speech with offensive words toward anyone or anything.
This is why in these two passages they limit themselves

to saying that they will ask God to restrain or rebuke the demons. Angels do not insult; they only love and bless. The teaching of Scripture is clear: *no one* should insult the demons. Actually, as Christians, we should not insult *anybody*—not even demons.

In exorcisms, demons are referred to as "serpent," "dragon," "unclean beast," etc., but these terms are not insults; they simply indicate what the demons are, even though it may torment them. The truth is proclaimed to them so that they cannot resist the suffering that hearing it produces in them and causes them to leave. While these terms are said with authority, they are always said without hate. Hate does not come from God.

64. What is demonic possession?

Demonic possession is the phenomenon in which a demon resides in the body of a human being. At specific moments, the demon can speak and move through the body without the person being able to prevent it.

Only the body is susceptible to demonic possession. A demon does not reside in—or in any way "possess"—the *soul* of the person. In all circumstances, the soul continues to be free and incapable of being possessed.

65. What are the essential characteristics of a possession?

A person should present the following characteristics for one to suspect demonic possession:

1. Sacred or religious objects present a range of sensations from repugnance to horror, from the least

expression of annoyance to the manifestation of anger or fury.

2. In the most extreme cases, this horror at the sacred leads to outbursts of fury, which is normally accompanied by blasphemy or insults directed toward the religious object that has been placed in proximity to the person.

3. In the most acute episodes of fury, the possessed loses consciousness. When the person regains consciousness, he remembers nothing; he has total amnesia. (Some, though, may be conscious and observe the episode, feeling as if an alien presence is operating in their bodies.) Nevertheless, even though the individual remembers nothing, he demonstrates a change of personality during this "anger crisis." A second personality emerges.

4. This second personality always has an evil character. It often happens that at those times a rolling of the eyes occurs, with the pupils turned upwards or downwards. There is often a twitching of facial muscles and hands, or rigidity in the body. In these moments of fury, the person articulates words full of hate and rage.

5. After the crisis passes, the person slowly returns to normalcy. This transition to normalcy is similar to the transition that is observed in the return from a state of hypnosis to a normal state of consciousness.

6. Outside of the periods of fury in which the second personality appears, the person lives a completely

normal life. This pathology does not noticeably affect him in his work or social relationships. The individual appears as a perfectly sane, normal person. He can perfectly distinguish between the real and "intra-psychic" worlds and is not aware of any delirious behavior.

7. In some cases, the possessed may experience sensory hallucinations, such as sporadically seeing shadows, feeling diffuse sensations on some part of their body, hearing creaking noises, or hearing voices.

66. Does the demon also possess the soul of the possessed?

No. As we have said, possession is a phenomenon that affects the body, not the soul. A possessed person's soul can be in the state of grace, and they can continue thinking and deciding freely. If a possessed person dies and is in the state of grace, he or she will go to heaven. So it is also perfectly licit for the possessed to receive Holy Communion. In some cases this will be possible, but in other cases it may be impossible for the person to even enter a church due to his possessed state.

The possessed person is not responsible, morally speaking, for what he says and does during the periods of fury when he loses consciousness and the "second personality" (that of the demon) emerges. But the possessed person, having free will, *is* responsible for what he or she does outside these unconscious periods.

67. What is the most practical way to know if someone is possessed?

Interviewing the person suspected of possession so that he can explain what is happening is an important first step. But we need to remember that a mental patient can read books on possession and try to imitate the signs that he has read about. That is why the best and most practical course of action to determine possession is to pray over him immediately after he has been interviewed.

It is prayer which will give us the assurance that one is dealing with a possession or not. If the person is possessed, he will start to twitch his hands and his face will gradually tense up. He will close his eyes, and if the priest lifts up his eyelids, he will see that the person's eyes are rolled back. If the prayer continues, the possessed may begin to scream or speak with an evil voice. In other cases, he lets out an evil laugh or begins to snort.

There are cases in which no trance is noticed, but rather the possessed person opens his eyes and talks at once. His voice is evil and anguished, and speaks to order those present to stop praying. Even though the trance is not noticeable, when he returns to normal he will remember nothing.

In some cases, the emergence of a second personality is not observed during the trance state. The only thing that is perceived externally is that the person rolls his eyes and remains motionless. Sometimes, his hands or body may move only slightly. These are called "mute" demons because they do not speak. Though they do not speak for

an extended period, the person enters into a trance once
the exorcism rite has begun.

68. How can a demon hide his presence in the possessed?

This is a major theme in cases of possession, and the
following answer should be read very carefully by priests
who are going to be dedicated to the ministry of exorcism.
It is vitally important because many demons will try to
trick exorcists, leading them to believe that someone is not
possessed.

There are different tricks a demon can use to remain
undetected, depending on whether he is *clausus* (Latin
for "shut, closed") or *apertus* ("open"). If the demon is
clausus, he will first try to hide and not show himself.
Some can resist showing themselves for five minutes
or more. That is why it is important to speak to the
supposedly possessed person before blessing him to
determine whether it is a credible case of possession.
If the possession seems credible, the exorcist has
to insist in the prayer of blessing for more time. The
clausus demon, when he can no longer resist the power
of the prayer, will cause the possessed person to enter
into a trance in which he will then close his eyes and
roll them back under the eyelids. But he will not move
or seek attention. If the priest stops the blessing and
does not lift up the eyelids, the possessed person will
immediately return to normal, without remembering
anything, and the priest will be tricked into believing
that the person is not possessed.

If the demon is *apertus,* he will do exactly the opposite
from what has been explained about the *clausus*. The

apertus will open the person's eyes and say that what the possessed is suffering is merely psychological. He will laugh at the exorcist as he prays and will ask him what sort of foolish things he is reciting. The demon will challenge whether he is trying to convince himself that the person is possessed. Curiously, when the possessed regains consciousness and the exorcist asks him why he said such and such a thing, he will say that he remembers nothing.

When a priest prays over a person to discern if he is possessed, and mocking and scornful behaviour begins, the priest should ask him why he says such things. During this prayer, the possessed person is completely unaware of what is happening. It is normal for a person possessed by this type of demon to laugh at what the priest is doing. Afterward, he may even ask forgiveness, saying, "Sorry, but what you are doing seems so funny to me. It is foolishness." Though the possessed is already in a trance, he speaks in a completely normal voice with gestures and reactions that lead one to believe that it is the person himself (rather than a demon) speaking. But the priest should be suspicious—after all, if he has come to verify if the person is possessed, why should everything suddenly seem so funny that the person cannot control his laughing? Why would the person, now that the priest is praying over him, say his problems are really only psychological when he insisted before that he was suffering from a demon? And if he remembers nothing of what was said, then it is clearly a possession. This will become clearer as the exorcism proceeds.

Sometimes the demon uses this strategy even during the exorcism. It is interesting that the demon, after having understood the Latin prayers and having showed a profound repulsion to all things sacred, makes such a desperate attempt to convince those present with a normal voice that in reality what the person suffers from is just a mental sickness and that they should let him leave. If the exorcist insists, though, he again shows himself.

69. What are "hidden demons"?

The *abditi* (Latin for "hidden" or "secret") demons are those that hide in the interior of the possessed person without showing themselves in any way. The person notices a change in his life and feels strange things that make him suspect there is an external force that has entered him. He can even experience preternatural phenomena. But when the priest prays, the demon resists and gives no sign of being present.

In these cases, a person possessed by such a demon must pray much for weeks or months. Here, we mean prayer in general, i.e., there is no need for any specific prayer against the demon. Attending Mass, praying the Rosary, and speaking with God on a daily basis are sufficient to gradually cause these hidden demons to leave. At the start, it is as if they are deep in the interior of the person and are forced little by little towards the exterior by prayer. This is why someone who has been told by an exorcist that he is not possessed has the right to be examined again after a month has passed. It is a good idea for the person to be prayed over, albeit briefly, three or four times a month between each prayer.

There have been cases of possessed persons whose demons have hidden themselves so absolutely that no exorcist, regardless of his level of knowledge and experience, could have detected their presence. In these cases, something preternatural had happened previously before several witnesses to make one suspect that a possession had occurred. After much insistence, though, the demon cannot resist any longer and shows himself in all his rage and with all the signs that often appear in possession.

In some cases, *abditi* demons have been able to resist more than two hours of exorcism without giving the least sign of their presence. I have known cases in which the person did not even feel slightly bad during the exorcism. But the exorcist and the family were certain the person was possessed because of the things they had witnessed on previous occasions. Nevertheless, when an *abditus* demon cannot resist anymore and reveals his presence, he acts like all other demons do. This being said, an exorcist should not keep trying to exorcise a person for an extended period without some sign of possession. Though an exorcist can affirm in this sense that someone is possessed without a doubt, affirming that someone is *not* possessed is not so easy. They can only affirm that the person does not show any *signs* of possession. Nevertheless, as a general norm, a priest should strive to make the person feel calm by assuring him that there is no demon present. To work in any other way would be to leave the person in a state of continuous psychological restlessness. By clearly saying that someone does not *appear* possessed, one always leaves open the possibility of seeing him in the future if he asks.

I remember the case of a man who was certain he had seen lights enter his house through the window. I examined him but did not see any signs of possession. The problem was that the entire family had seen the phenomenon and confirmed his story. So I offered him the following conclusions:

1. If there were no witnesses to confirm his story, the issue was probably psychological in nature. But since his family also reported seeing the phenomenon, I had my doubts about a psychological cause.

2. He showed no signs of possession.

3. I recommended he do the following:

    a. Take the medication prescribed by his psychiatrist and follow all his recommendations.

    b. Go to Mass and pray the Rosary.

4. If it was a psychiatric problem, he was doing well seeking medical treatment and should see some improvement; if the problem was demonic in nature, though, God would hear his prayers. Of course, he could return to see me again after a month or two.

The recommendations I offer above would work for all cases in which the diagnosis is not clear.

After some time, the man did return to see me. It became clear that this was a case of possession. Unfortunately, cases such as this do happen. I say "unfortunately" because I wish that everything about possession were simpler and clearer, but this subject has the level of complexity God has willed for it. No more, no less.

70. What prayer should a priest pray to determine if someone is possessed?

A priest can bless the person with prayers from the ritual of blessings or with prayers made up in the moment. He can use the following simple phrases easily learned by heart: *In nomine Iesu, exorcizo te. In nomine Iesu, dic nomen tuum. In nomine Iesu, si es hic, manifesta te.* (In the name of Jesus, I exorcize you. In the name of Jesus, say your name. In the name of Jesus, if you are present, show yourself.)

The exorcist always speaks to the demon with the authority of Christ. Rather than asking the demon anything, the priest *orders* or *commands* him in the name of Jesus. Speaking in Latin is helpful because the person does not know when the exorcist is addressing the demon. If the person shows no signs of a trance or that a second personality is emerging, then he is not possessed. In ninety-five percent of possession cases, the demon shows himself after a few seconds of prayer. But, as we have already discussed, there are certain demons that can remain hidden for a long time and resist the prayer with all their strength. In such cases, the priest needs to pray with a little more insistence. Normally, only a few additional minutes of prayer are necessary to get the demon to reveal himself.

Since there are many different types of demons, the priest should ask God to enlighten him. He also needs to follow his intuition. If there is something that makes him suspect a demon is present, he can be more insistent in his commands (though, as we have said, only a few minutes are usually necessary). When he is blessing the person, it is very important that the priest be very focused in his prayer. The greater the exorcist's concentration, the greater the strength of the prayer and the quicker the demon will manifest himself. It is helpful for the priest to keep his eyes closed in prayer so he is not distracted by looking at the person. But, during this time, someone else should be watching the possessed in case he attempts to throw himself on the priest and disrupt the exorcism.

While the priest is concentrating on the prayer, he could look at the person's eyes for a moment. In some cases the person's eyes close as he enters into a trance. In other cases, the demon looks through them with an evil look. If the priest observes this look, he should then command the demon to show himself.

71. What are the causes of possession?

The chief causes of possession are the following:

1. Making a pact with the devil (or demons).

2. Taking part in spiritualist sessions, satanic cults, or esoteric rites.

3. Offering one's child to Satan.

4. Being the victim of witchcraft (i.e., a spell).

Possession is not contagious. Living with a possessed person or being in his presence does not carry with it any danger of becoming possessed yourself. Only one who opens the door to the devil—or, in the case of a spell, is the victim of one who opens such a door—gets possessed. Many people think that sin causes possession, but it does not. One has to expressly open a door for a demon to enter. Sin, even grave sin, is one thing, possession another. One does not necessarily lead to the other. One could be possessed without being in mortal sin, while another in mortal sin is not possessed.

It may seem fitting that one who voluntarily opens the door to a demon could be possessed, but what about cases of possession resulting from a spell? In such cases, one becomes possessed because someone else performs a ritual and directs demonic power his way. We need to remember that possession only affects the body, not the soul. As such, there is no problem with respect to divine justice. In the same way that one can hire the Mafia to kill someone, so too God sometimes allows this evil with respect to the body. Possession only occurs if God allows it. The particular rites that are performed are irrelevant; if God does not allow the evil, nothing will take place. Of course, the greater the spiritual life of a person, the more protected he will be against all these influences of the Evil One.

The fact that even those in a state of grace can be possessed through no fault of their own has been proven time and again over the centuries. God permits this evil because many times the evils that occur to a person's body in possession are a source of blessings for the soul. After being possessed, a person remains much more thankful to God and has a much stronger spiritual life for the whole of life.

On the other hand, it can be said that those who cast spells against the health of other people or to get them possessed do not normally do this for very long. They typically experience divine punishment in short order. Few things attract God's justice as much as practicing spells against others. This type of person can only practice their evil arts for a short time before God takes their life and calls them to His terrible judgement.

72. Why do demons possess people?

The demons know that possessing a person carries with it the risk that this possession may bring about a greater good in his or her soul in the end. Given this risk, then, why do they do it?

While it would undoubtedly be more convenient for a demon not to possess anyone, he does this for one simple reason: to cause suffering. Remember: demons seek to make people suffer, and with possession they can accomplish this in a very direct way. Over the long term, a particular possession may ultimately thwart the plans of the devil by bringing about a deeper devotion to God in the possessed. But in the here and now, it causes the person to suffer—and a demon cannot resist causing certain suffering in the present. What was said in a previous answer regarding why the devil could not resist tempting Jesus is equally valid here. To resist temptation, one needs virtue, and we cannot expect a demon to be virtuous. He always seeks the benefits in the here and now; he is a slave of his own passions and impulses.

73. Why does God allow demonic possessions to occur?

While this is ultimately a mystery, we can see that God allows possession for the following reasons:

- Possession demonstrates the truth of the Catholic faith.

- Possession punishes sinners who seek a relationship with evil.

- Possession can be a spiritual benefit.

- Possession can produce wholesome teachings for humanity.

Since God allows physical illness, which often brings about an increase in faith, there are even more reasons for Him to permit a reality—possession—that often brings about an even deeper faith. Possession is a phenomenon in which the power of God, Christ, and the Church is clearly demonstrated. It is like an open window through which we can look at the world of hatred and demonic suffering. It is an open window through which we can glimpse some of the invisible power of angelic natures. And the good that comes from all of this normally affects those present for the rest of their lives.

I say "normally" since merely being present at an exorcism does not guarantee a deeper faith. There are those who, after witnessing an exorcism, attribute everything they have witnessed to natural (or unknown) causes. We shouldn't be surprised at this. After all, there were people in Jesus' time who did not believe in Him even after witnessing His miracles. We have to understand that, regardless of what we see, grace is required for faith. If a person freely decides to resist grace's interior and invisible invitation, he could see the heavens open and hear God speaking to him from on high through the clouds and still believe he was having a hallucination. It is not what we experience that ignites the interior of our immortal souls with the flame of faith; it is the grace of God.

74. What is the difference between schizophrenia and possession?

Simply put, the following distinctions can be made between the mental illness of schizophrenia and possession:

- Schizophrenia has a natural cause; possession has a demonic cause.

- Schizophrenia occurs as a result of organic, psychiatric reasons; possession normally occurs following participation in occult, esoteric rites.

- Schizophrenia is treated by psychiatric science, including medication; possession is resolved by exorcism.

- In schizophrenia no extraordinary phenomena are observed; in possession, extraordinary phenomena are often seen.

75. What extraordinary phenomena occur in a possession?

When a trance state is present or a demonic personality appears, we can be certain that we are dealing with a true case of demonic possession. There are cases of possession, however, in which other extraordinary phenomena are manifested. The most frequent phenomena are:

- The person suddenly understands *foreign (or even "dead") languages he has never studied.* Regardless of the person's age or intelligence, he will obey orders given in Latin, Greek, Hebrew, and other languages, even when used simultaneously. Sometimes the possessed will speak to those present in these unknown languages, though this is less common.

- The possessed displays *abnormal physical strength,* sometimes over the course of several hours. Sometimes the person is even able to perform acts that are usually impossible, such as lifting several people at once.

- The person demonstrates a *knowledge of hidden things.*

- Perhaps the most extraordinary phenomenon of all— and the most infrequent—is *levitation.*

Some cases of possession, however, manifest no extraordinary phenomena at all.

76. Why are there fewer cases of possession now than in Jesus' day?

Actually, the assumption behind this question is very difficult to prove since we do not have any historical statistics on the matter. Many people suppose that after Christ shed His blood on Calvary, the power of the devil over the world was broken, and this is why there are fewer cases of demonic possession today. There were many rites in ancient times in which spirits were invoked that contributed to possession. As a result, it seems logical to assume that possession was much more frequent in pagan Babylon than in medieval Europe. It was not the redemption of Christ per se that caused demonic possession to decline but the abandonment of rites that invoked evil spirits once the Church became dominant in society. Christ has redeemed us, but if demons are invoked, possession can still occur.

77.   What types of demons appear in possessions?

As we have said previously, there are two principal types of demons that cause two distinct types of possession: the *clausi* and the *aperti*. A *clausus* demon causes the possessed to close his eyes (with them rolled back) when entering into a trance. An *apertus* demon causes the possessed to keep his eyes open while in a trance, giving looks of anger and rage, and speaking a great deal. The *aperti* are loquacious and violent, and the possessed person often needs to be held down during the exorcism; some *clausi* will speak after some time of prayer, always without opening their eyes, but others are completely mute.

We can diagram the two types in the following manner:

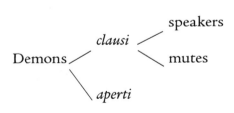

Even though one is dealing with different types of demons, an exorcism begins in the same manner. Afterwards, the exorcist will notice what torments each one in a particular way and one will focus on that.

The *abditi* demons spoken of previously are not, in reality, a distinct type of demon; they are simply demons who hide themselves within the person. Once they have been forced to reveal themselves, they will act like the *clausi* or *aperti*.

78. What happens if the possessed person dies before being freed of the demon?

Many people think that if a possessed person dies while being possessed he will go to hell. This is incorrect. If the person is in the state of grace, he will go to heaven. Remember: possession affects only the person's body. Once the person is dead, of course, the demon leaves and does not enter into another.

79. Can the soul of a condemned person possess someone?

Yes, in my opinion, the souls of the condemned can possess someone in exactly the same way as a demon. Some possessed persons, when they are in a trance, insist during the exorcism that they are not demons but deceased human beings. The exorcist must determine if they are lying, and that is why this is a debated question among exorcists. Nevertheless, one has to take into account that, no matter how much the exorcist insists in the name of Jesus that the possessed tell the truth, they do not yield in this assertion. They will yield in everything (kissing the cross, praising God, etc.), but they insist that they are human beings who have been condemned to hell and not demons. If they obey in everything but remain firm only in this assertion, it is reasonable to believe that they are telling the truth.

80. Can possessed people kill?

Since a demon takes possession of a person's body and can move and talk by means of it, many people ask if a demon can cause the possessed person to kill. Experience teaches us that the possessed can do many things while in a trance state, e.g., remain still with their eyes rolled back, have convulsions, and shout. But a demon does not normally cause the person to physically injure himself or others for one simple reason: God does not ordinarily permit it. The demon possessing the person wants to do all the evil it can, but God puts limits on the amount of evil it can do.

This being said, if a possessed person has natural suicidal tendencies, then there is a real danger that, while in the trance state, the demon may try to urge him to throw himself from a window or do some other suicidal act. Such persons should be carefully watched, and the permission of the bishop to perform an exorcism should be secured as soon as possible.

Even though some possessed people, while in the state of trance, can act aggressively toward a particular individual, it is very rare that they do any real harm. Their aggression is usually limited to screaming, looking at the person with hatred, or making their hands look like claws. It is extremely unusual for the possessed to actually try to harm another person physically; on those rare occasions when they try to do this, they fail in their attempts. It is as if an outside force is preventing them from fulfilling this desire.

81. Are serial killers possessed?

It is commonly asked whether serial killers are possessed. The answer is simple: some are, some are not. Some are possessed, many suffer from various psychiatric disorders, and—as amazing as it may sound—the remainder are neither mentally ill nor possessed; they have simply chosen an evil path.

We sometimes hear media reports of horrendous murders committed by certain serial killers or members of satanic cults who seem to exhibit the characteristics of demonic possession. In these cases, it is not always easy to distinguish what was done consciously and what was done unconsciously. Normally, the murderer seems to be conscious at the start of the crime, but he gradually enters into an unconscious frenzy in which he does not seem to have control of his actions. These are crimes committed by people who are truly evil in their conscious state while at the same time possessed. So it is difficult to determine whether or not they were in a state of possession when they committed their crime.

Of course, even if a criminal is possessed, this does not alter his responsibility before the law. Since there is no legal recognition of demonic possession, a serial killer is often considered by the law to be mentally ill (or legally *insane*). Nonetheless, society cannot leave his acts unpunished on the grounds that "an invisible force" caused him to kill. No court could accept such an acquittal as it would render the entire legal process insecure.

VI. EXORCISM AND THE PATH TO DELIVERANCE

82. What is an exorcism?

The rite of exorcism is the official ritual of the Church in which a demon is ordered in the name of Christ to leave the body of a possessed person (see CCC 1673). While the ecclesiastical rite of exorcism contains many secondary parts (e.g., the litany of the saints, the liturgy of the Word, the Lord's Prayer, etc.), its essence is the casting out of the demon. The prayers directed to God are *deprecatory*—that is to say, God is begged for His assistance in casting out the demon. Nothing is ever *asked* of the demon; rather, he is *ordered* to depart by the name of the Redeemer. If an exorcism does not have a "casting out," it is not a true exorcism.

83. In the gospels, could exorcism be just a symbol of liberation from evil?

No. To deny the reality of exorcism and to hold that it is merely a symbol of deliverance from evil is a heresy. The constant tradition of the Church has affirmed the possibility of demonic possession. The saints, the Church Fathers and Doctors, and the practice of the Church in East and West throughout history are unanimous in stating that possession is the domination of the demon on a human body.

The New Testament clearly distinguishes between illness and possession, and this is especially so in the gospels. For example, Matthew 8:16 states, "He cast out the spirits with a word, and healed all who were sick"; and Mark 1:32, 34 makes a similar distinction: "They brought to him all who were sick or possessed with demons ... and he healed many who were sick with various diseases, and cast out many demons." It is always clear that possession is caused by an evil spiritual being. It is a phenomenon so distinct that a special Greek verb is used whenever Jesus goes to expel a demon—*exorkizo* ("to conjure"). Such individuals are not called "ill" or "sick" but *daimonizomai* ("demon-possessed"). Possession is not *cured*; rather, the possessed person is *freed*. This group of people that appear in the four gospels shout and have crises of agitation. Jesus will address himself to *daimonia* in an imperative way, giving orders without showing any compassion at all.

84. What is the difference between an exorcism and a prayer of deliverance from a demonic oppression?

An exorcism is a liturgical rite that is carried out on people who are possessed. Deliverance is a series of private prayers prayed over people who suffer from some type of demonic influence.

The liturgical rite of exorcism is already predetermined; it requires authorization on the part of the bishop and should be carried out only when one is certain that a person is possessed by a demonic spirit.

The prayer of deliverance can be long or it can last less than fifteen minutes. It can be done by a prayer group or by a priest; either way, it is a private prayer. In other words, it is not a liturgical prayer and it can also be improvised. This private prayer of deliverance can be done even if there is only a suspicion of a harmful demonic influence, to whatever degree and however weak it may be.

In an exorcism, the priest prays that the possessed person be freed from the devil. In a deliverance prayer, we ask God to set a person free from some degree of demonic influence, including what some have referred to as "clinging spirits." Often, when we experience a wound—either self-imposed due to sin or from some outside force or person—demonic spirits can "attach" to the wound and prevent healing. We can also experience unhealthy "soul ties" to people, through sexual contact and emotionally abusive relationships. Demonic spirits can "cling" to these as well and, thus, prevent healing, which is a primary aim of such spirits. Although our sin is forgiven, the demons want to prevent deep emotional and spiritual healing. Deliverance prayers can break the bonds of such spirits and bring about a greater freedom for us than if we did not have such prayers said.

In an exorcism, the priest is certain that the person is possessed. Meanwhile, in a deliverance prayer, the priest is not sure as to the extent of the demonic oppression.

85. What is the best way to organize the ministry of exorcist?

The ideal way to organize the ministry of exorcist is to ensure that there are a sufficient number of well-trained priests.

As it is not an obligation that every diocese have its own exorcist, it may be best to concentrate the ministry in an archdiocese (or the principal see of a region or country) rather than in each suffragan or smaller diocese. It needs to be clear, though, that an exorcism can be performed in a given diocese only with the permission of its bishop (see *CCC* 1673).

The most delicate part of this ministry is not the exorcism per se, but rather the discernment of possession. On the one hand, if we mistakenly conclude a person is not possessed when he truly is, we may inflict terrible suffering on him with a lifetime of consequences. On the other hand, if we conclude that a person is possessed while he really is not, the Church will be discredited. Since the media loves to dwell on negative publicity regarding the Church, just one error of this kind can have tragic consequences.

For this reason, it is better to concentrate specialists in discernment in archdioceses. Once a case of suspected possession has proven credible, the archdiocesan specialist can consult with the diocese in which the possessed person resides so that an authorized priest can proceed with an exorcism.

Though it is sufficient that only one specialist tend to a particular case, it is preferable that three exorcists be involved in the discernment team. The three priests should be of different ages to ensure that, if one dies, not all knowledge dies with him. Regardless of how much of the knowledge of discernment is put on paper, nothing can take the place of experience. For this reason, it is good that an older, more experienced exorcist teach a younger exorcist.

After it has been proven that the case at hand is a real possession and the proper episcopal authorization has been granted, it is ideal to have a team of five to ten laypeople to assist during the exorcism by praying and helping hold down the possessed. The prayer of this team of laypeople who assist at the exorcism is greater than that of the priest alone.

It is not necessary for the same team of priests who discerned the case to also perform the exorcism. As has been already said, the actual exorcism is easier than the action of discernment. For the exorcism, the official manual is enough. But there is no manual that can discern the true cases from the false ones; the accumulated experience of specialists is needed.

In conclusion, the best way to organize the ministry of exorcist in an archdiocese is with three key groups: 1) specialists in charge of discerning true cases of possession; 2) exorcists who perform the actual exorcisms; and 3) a team of laypeople who assist with prayers and helps restrain the person (if necessary) during the exorcism. Since the possessed normally needs a true catechesis to help him grow closer to Christ, within this third group of lay assistants there can also be a more established group who spiritually assist the possessed person and his family.

Some of these assistants may in time gather sufficient experience so that they could become consulters. If a lay assistant is also a Catholic psychiatrist who understands the spiritual life well, his or her opinion will seem to be the most accurate in order to discern cases. This being said, though, in my experience there is nothing better than common sense and a devout spiritual life.

86. Is a psychiatric evaluation necessary before proceeding with an exorcism?

No. The Church does not usually require a psychiatric evaluation of an individual prior to proceeding with an exorcism. No such requirement appears in any normative text on the subject. Why? A psychiatric evaluation can only speak of *possibilities*. If the exorcist is *certain* of possession, then why would he need a psychiatric evaluation? In not a few cases, it has been shown that psychiatric illness coexists with demonic possession, but the two realities are distinct. Mental illness does not preclude the possibility of possession.

87. Why does a priest need permission from the bishop to proceed with an exorcism?

In the early Church, a priest did not need the permission of his bishop to exorcise. The ministry was exercised whenever it seemed opportune. By the fifth century, though, an ecclesiastical norm was established that no one could perform an exorcism without the authorization of the bishop. In the year 416, Pope Innocent I wrote a letter to Bishop Gubbio stating:

> You should have a charitable attitude to those baptised, whom after baptism are possessed by the devil, because of some vice or sin. For this

reason, a priest or deacon can be designated. To perform [the exorcism] is not licit without the order from the bishop. *[De his vero baptizatis, qui postea a demonio, vitio aliquo aut peccato interveniente, arripiuntur, est sollicita dilectio tua, si a presbitero vel diacono possint aut debeant designari. Quod hoc, nisi episcopus praeceperit non licet.]* (PL XX, 557- 558)

Why did the Church impose this requirement? Because it came to see that this field requires a special prudence. Also, the issue is delicate enough that an imprudent act of a clergyman could especially harm the supposedly possessed person and cause harm to the prestige of the Church in general. For this reason, the Church opted to establish a special vigilance in this ministry. It is interesting to note that in the East this ministry was exercised as a charismatic activity, which did not need the expressed permission of the bishop.

88. What is demonic infestation?

Demonic infestation is the phenomenon in which a demon possesses a *place*, such as a house or building, or an *object*. A demon, by possessing a place, can move things at will and cause various noises and smells. Infestation never causes the possession of any of the *people* who live there. An infestation may occur in a particular place due to some esoteric or satanic rites being performed with frequency. Such infestation may result from a hex, spell, or curse, or from voodoo or witchcraft. To end the infestation of a place, the rite of exorcism lists several specific prayers that need to be prayed.

A priest should not be too quick to believe the testimony of strange phenomena in a house unless there are at least two corroborating eyewitnesses. In the case of a suspected possession of a person, a priest can pray and confirm the presence of a demon. In the case of infestation, however, nothing happens when he prays in the suspected place. Therefore, everything depends on what is reported to him. This is why there is no way to establish a true infestation with certainty without several corroborating testimonies about the extraordinary events that have been witnessed.

In these cases, the priest can bless the house and encourage the family to pray together every day. They can pray the Rosary, read the Bible together, sprinkle holy water in the various rooms, come together before a holy image and beg protection, etc. The persistent prayer of a family, over the course of several weeks or months, can completely destroy the demonic infestation in their house.

89. Can animals be infested?

Yes, but this is extremely rare. The possession of animals is also a form of demonic infestation. If it were to occur, sacrificing the animal would cause the demon to leave and nothing more would happen. Once the demon leaves the animal (because it is dead), it would not possess anyone else.

Very few cases of animal infestation have been referred to me. I do know of one case in which a house was infested. A priest went to do an exorcism of the place, and it was successfully liberated from demonic infestation. After this, though, the family dog began to behave strangely. Every time the front door was opened, the dog would run out and stop in the middle of the street. The family would go out and get the dog, but it was eventually struck by a car.

Infestation of an object can occur only if the object has been used in a spell or incantation. We know that a particular object is infested when it causes certain demonic activities—e.g., things inexplicably move, or there are unexplainable noises or bad smells—wherever it is placed. In such cases, the object must be burned after being sprinkled with holy water. The ashes should then be buried.

90. Who can be an exorcist?

It is commonly believed that a priest must be holy and virtuous to be an exorcist, and this is undoubtedly ideal; the more virtuous he is, the better. But, strictly speaking, *any* priest can perform the rite of exorcism. Even priests who are not the most edifying can expel demons without difficulty, though the exorcism may take a little longer. While it may seem scandalous to some, even a priest in a state of mortal sin can perform an exorcism and successfully expel a demon. Why? Because the rite of exorcism is a liturgical prayer of the Church in which the power of prayer, the power of the priesthood, and the power of the name of Jesus are used. As with the ministry of the sacraments, it works *ex opere operato*, i.e., independently of the worthiness of the minister. The holiness of the priest is helpful but is unnecessary.

Even though holiness is not absolutely necessary for exorcism, common sense is. Common sense is the only thing that the Church cannot supplement—a priest either has it or he does not. In addition to having common sense, the exorcist should be willing to dedicate the time, interest, and tenderness necessary to fulfill this ministry well. Though he may have wisdom and virtue, if he performs exorcisms in a hurry and without attending to the needs of the possessed, he will be a poor exorcist. In this case, a priest of lesser virtue with great attentiveness is preferable.

91.   Is there a danger of pride for an exorcist?

Yes, and this danger is very great. Exorcism is a ministry that, if practiced regularly, attracts a general admiration and the most profound gratitude from those who have been freed from possession. On the other hand, the continuous exercise of this ministry gives the exorcist a very specialized and deep knowledge of demons that cannot be learned in any book or in school.

To compensate for this potential source of pride, God normally allows the exorcist to suffer the misunderstanding and ridicule of many of his brother priests. As such, the exorcist works all his life between being admired and thanked by some and bitterly despised and persecuted by others. This helps him grow in the virtue of humility.

Every exorcist knows fellow clergymen who think he is crazy and that his work is a danger to the reputation and image of the Church. Unfortunately, I do not know of any exorcist who has not had to suffer at the hands of priests determined to speak about and end the "scandal" of "medieval superstition" (i.e., exorcism) for the "good of the Church."

Whoever is named to the ministry of exorcist should not think that the persecution he suffers is merely the result of misunderstanding, i.e., that it will last only until others see the fruits of exorcism and the good sense with which he works. Urged on by Satan, who wants to discourage the exorcist at all costs, persecution will come, regardless of how dedicated or holy he is or how much common sense he has.

Unfortunately, the persecution exorcists endure is not something that happens occasionally or only to some. Everyone who serves as an exorcist will experience it to one degree or another. God desires that this ministry always be done from the Cross. If a priest is not willing to bear this burden, he should not accept this ministry.

92. Are there exorcisms outside of the Catholic Church?

Yes. True and effective exorcisms are performed in the different Christian confessions. On the one hand, the Eastern Orthodox churches maintain apostolic succession, in which their bishops and priests are validly ordained and, as such, possess a true sacramental power. On the other hand, the various Protestant churches, though they do not possess a valid ministerial priesthood, profess faith in Christ and in the power of His name. With just such weapons, the devil can be expelled.

God, in His wisdom, has not desired to place too many conditions on the most essential Christian practices for them to be valid. For example, baptism, by which one enters into the Christian faith, is normally considered valid in all Christian traditions (provided that the Trinitarian formula given by Jesus is followed: "I baptize you in the name of the Father, and of the Son, and of the Holy Spirit"). Likewise, Jesus knew the great suffering demonic possession would cause to those afflicted by it, and He did not want to establish strict conditions to be followed to make exorcisms effective.

In Orthodox Christianity, exorcisms are performed in a manner very similar to those of the Roman Catholic ritual. In the Pentecostal churches of Protestantism, exorcisms normally consist of a group of faithful who get together to praise God, and, in the midst of these praises, order the demon again and again to leave the person in the name of Jesus. The faith of those present and the power of Jesus' name are sufficient to cause the demons to leave.

Aside from the Pentecostal tradition, the major "mainline" Protestant churches (e.g., Lutheran, Anglican, Presbyterian) no longer emphasize the reality of demonic possession and no longer practice exorcism. It seems strange that these followers of Christ do not know how to deal with cases of oppression from the Evil One. Once a tradition cuts itself off from centuries of Christian belief and practice, new methods for dealing with the devil cannot be invented from scratch.

93. Why do some exorcisms last so long?

Since not all the demons are from the same hierarchy, not all have the same power.

As a result, some demons are more difficult to expel than others. Those demons who have angelic natures belonging to the highest choirs are the most difficult to drive out of a body. Satan and Lucifer are the most difficult to exorcise. No matter how holy the exorcist, an exorcism of such a powerful demon takes time. We can see a parallel here in the world of medicine, where heart or brain surgery is more complex and takes longer than merely cosmetic surgery.

We can see that even in the Bible some exorcisms were more difficult—and lengthy—than others. In Mark 9:17-18, for example, we read how the apostles could not expel a demon from a young boy. When they later ask Jesus why they could not cast it out, Jesus responds, "This kind cannot be driven out by anything but prayer and fasting" (Mk 9:28, 29). In exorcism, as with any ministry, there is a distinction to be made between *power* and *authority*: "And [Jesus] called the Twelve together and gave them power and authority over all demons" (Lk 9:1). This distinction is seen in Jesus' response to them in Mark 9:29—the apostles had full authority but needed to increase their power over the demons by growing in holiness (i.e., through "prayer and fasting").

Conversely, in Mark 9:38, we read of a man who had power over the demons even though he had no apostolic authority: "Teacher, we saw a man casting out demons in your name, and we forbade him, because he was not following us."

94. How does one know that the last demon has left the person?

Given the fact that the possessed may have several demons,

the question of how one determines when the last demon has left arises. When a demon leaves, the person remains at peace, recovers consciousness, and opens his eyes. He may even feel a spiritual happiness. The exorcist should pray for the person for two or three more minutes. If a demon is still inside, the person will fall back into a trance or the demon will become furious. If the person remains conscious, he should be asked if he feels anything. If the answer is no, then everyone present should kneel down and thank the Lord for freeing the person from the demon. They should also thank the angels and saints for their help and intercession.

If a priest believes that every demon has left but this, in fact, is not the case, no great harm would be done. The possessed would simply call him again, saying that some of the symptoms that made him ask for an exorcism in the first place are still present. The exorcist would then need to repeat the prayers to drive out the last demon (or demons).

95. Can one who has been possessed be "re-possessed" after being exorcised?

The possessed person and their family ask this question with much desperation during the process of exorcism. I can categorically answer them in the negative—they will not be possessed again. If the person lives in the grace of God, prays, and goes to Mass and regular confession (i.e., once a month or even more frequently), he has nothing to fear since he is protected; the evil cannot enter again. On the other hand, if the freed person returns to his old life of sin, he could be possessed again. If he is repossessed, this will be by more and worse demons.

We need to leave the newly liberated in a very tranquil state, telling him that if he lives a Christian life, a demon could not enter him again, even if it wanted to. One also needs to assure him that a demon will not return even if he should commit one or more mortal sins. He is in danger only if he reverts to living in a state of sin (i.e., to an ongoing situation of estrangement from God).

For example, I know of a lady who had been released from all her demons. A few days later, she called me saying that she felt bad—the feelings of oppression in her chest she had felt before (as well as other symptoms) had returned. I was very surprised because I was certain that all the demons had been cast out of her. She assured me that, since she had been freed, she was praying a lot, reading the Bible, and doing other spiritual things. I laid my hands on and prayed over her. She did not go into a trance but did feel the weight on her chest grow stronger and stronger until it gradually began to recede. As the prayer was going on (which lasted no more than five minutes), the oppression she was feeling became increasingly weaker until it disappeared completely. She has had no problems since then.

What had happened in this case? This was clearly demonic influence. The demon had left but then tried to enter into her again. It could not re-enter because she was protected by the armor of the spiritual life. The demon could not possess her; no matter how much I prayed, she never entered into a trance. The prayers broke this influence that the devil had over her body and the demon was driven away forever, never to return.

This is the clearest example I have seen of a demon trying

to return to a newly liberated person's body and being unable. The spiritual life, though we do not see it, is a true and authentic protective armor against the Evil One.

96. What happens if, in an exorcism, the demons do not leave?

If weeks or months go by without any demons being cast out, this could mean that the possessed person is not following the exorcist's direction. Before the first session of the exorcism, the exorcist should advise the possessed to pray, go to Mass, confess, and strive to live in accord with the Ten Commandments.

Some people approach an exorcist as they would a doctor. They think that an exorcism is similar to taking prescription medicine: the medicine will cure their illness and they can continue to live as before. But if one wants to be exorcised, he must make a life change and strive to fulfill all of the teachings of Jesus. If not, a demon may not leave because it has something to hold on to—and, if the demon is expelled, it may return. If the possessed is unwilling to abandon sin, the priest should suspend the exorcism sessions until the person agrees to obey his instructions. For example, if the person is living in an illicit union, he needs to first understand why he must put his life in order before God. Good intentions are worth nothing; the law of God is objective and must be obeyed. If the exorcism is begun before the person makes the life changes he needs to, it will have no effect. As we have said, if a demon has something to hold on to, it will not leave.

Normally, a longer-than-usual exorcism is the result of some hidden disobedience by the possessed to the instructions of the exorcist. If the person seems sincere and is following the exorcist's instructions, then the best remedy is to bring in another priest to see if he will be more successful. A less-experienced exorcist could be doing things that are ineffective with a particular demon. It may be useful to try again with a priest who has more experience.

97. What makes a demon leave the body during an exorcism?

There are three things that can make a demon leave a person's body:

1. The demon itself decides to leave.

2. The priestly power forces it to leave.

3. An angel sent by God forces it to leave.

Weaker demons normally leave on their own. Sacred things and prayer torture them, and the moment arrives when they decide to leave to avoid suffering. Sometimes when they leave they say things like, "I am leaving. You have not cast me out; I leave of my own will."

Stronger demons, though, at first refuse to leave no matter how much they are tortured. Exorcising these demons takes more time, but the order of the exorcist forces them out. During the exorcism, they get slowly weaker and end up being cast out by the power of the prayer.

Demons of the highest rank, though they also suffer terribly during an exorcism, refuse to leave unless an angel comes to cast them out. At a certain point during the deprecatory prayer, God sends an angel to free the person. Toward the end of the exorcism, an invisible fight between angel and demon occurs. The possessed person looks at a specific place and tries to scratch and hit those present. It is then that the worst convulsions and screams take place. Even though the exorcist may be quiet, the angel is present and the possessed is freed by means of his intervention.

98. What is a curse?

A *curse* is an action that is done to harm another with the help of demons. There are specific curses to kill, to cause one to be possessed, to make things go bad in business, to make someone sick, etc. As we have already stated, curses are effective only if God allows them to have effect. The more one prays, the more one will be protected against these things.

The former rite of exorcism states in its introduction: "Do command the demon to tell you if it remains in that body by some magic work, signs, or curse instruments; if there are such things that the possessed has eaten they have to be vomited out. If they are somewhere outside of the body then it has to be revealed. When they are found they have to be completely burnt."

If a possessed person vomits up a cursed object, it must be burnt. It is better if the exorcist does not touch it, but if he does, he should continue praying while doing so. His hands must be washed with holy water. If not, these types of objects may cause him health problems for some time.

99. Are curses really effective?

Many people ask if curses are truly effective. Well, the first thing that has to be said is that whoever *does* the curse—as well as the person who may have asked for the curse to be done—will be the first one affected by the demonic. Without a doubt, they will suffer some type of demonic influence, possession, or sickness. The evil they wish on another will come back to them. A demon is never invoked in vain.

But is a curse effective against the person to whom it is directed? This depends on the will of God. That is to say, it is the same as with accidents, illnesses, or misfortunes. During our time on earth, God allows us to experience both good and evil because this life is a period of trial, of purification. Of course, the person who prays and lives in God's grace is protected. The more one prays and lives a spiritual life, the more one is protected.

How can we know if someone is the victim of a curse? In most cases there is no way of knowing since demonic action is invisible. It is only certain in the cases of possession or demonic influence in which visible signs are evident to the exorcist. It is also possible to deduce that a particular evil is the fruit of a curse when this evil is accompanied by preternatural evil events. But, apart from external evidence of the action of demons, one can never know if something comes from natural causes or not.

100. What can be done to counteract a curse?

Though it is often impossible to know for sure that a curse is present, what can a person do if he strongly suspects a curse has been done against him? If he is truly under a curse, the only way to remove it is to do just the opposite. In other words, if a person has invoked a demon to do evil, then one has to invoke God to protect, help, and bless him. Good is always stronger than evil.

When people come to my parish saying that they are suffering from a curse, I tell them that it is impossible to prove demonic causality except in rare cases. But if they really suffer from a curse, the only remedy is to do the following:

- Pray the Rosary

- Read the Bible

- Speak with God every day

- Attend Mass frequently, even daily

- Place a blessed crucifix and an image of the Blessed Virgin Mary in one's house

- Make the sign of the cross with holy water daily

If the evil a person is suffering is from a demon, it will go away as a result of these devotions. If nothing changes, however, then the evil the person is suffering is not caused by a curse. Also, if a priest is an exorcist and suspects a curse, he can pray a prayer of deliverance and this will remedy the situation.

On some occasions, though, a demon causes the evil—sickness, for example—and departs. In these cases, the person's medical problems are the result of a curse but the exorcist sees that there is no demonic influence remaining. The person's illness, then, is like any other sickness and needs to be cured by medical treatment. There is no further need for supernatural remedies.

101. What is a charm?

Whereas a *curse* is used to harm someone through the power of demons, a *charm* is used to obtain something *positive* with the help of demons—for example, to get someone to fall in love, to make things go well in business, or to get someone promoted. Of course, demons cannot really give people these things; they can only tempt and influence other people to help bring them about. As such, charms do not normally work. Nevertheless, they can lead to some type of demonic influence, even possession. This is the case for the person who does (or asks for) the charm, and sometimes also for the person to whom the charm is directed.

During an exorcism, the object of a curse or charm can be discovered. It must be destroyed. Even if nothing is found, the prayer to God will destroy the influence of any demonic object that might be present.

102. What is the difference between white and black magic?

In popular language, *white magic* is said to be magic that is used for good, whereas *black magic* is used for evil. But both types of "magic" are useless. Strictly speaking, any paranormal effect achieved through magic is accomplished through the intervention of demons, not as a result of a particular person's "magical" powers. Even if those who practice magic—witches, sorcerers, seers, etc.— deny it (or are even unaware of it), the devil is behind all their works. And the very magic they practice in the end opens them up to demonic influence and even possession.

103. Can psychics and mediums see the future with the intervention of demons?

No, for two important reasons: First, as we have mentioned, demons themselves do not know the future but can only deduce possibilities; and second, demons seek to do evil to us and, even if they had knowledge of the future, they would not help us by revealing it. That being said, as an exception, they can reveal some concrete future possibility so that a person can become addicted to consulting a psychic or medium.

A Christian should never for any reason consult a psychic. Consulting such a person is objectively a grave sin because, in the words of the *Catechism*, "recourse to mediums ... conceal[s] a desire for power over time, history, and, in the last analysis, other human beings ... they contradict the honor, respect, and loving fear that we owe God alone" (*CCC* 2116). Also, one should never advise a possessed person to consult a medium or psychic. What a priest cannot see with theological knowledge he should not try to replace with the false science of these seers.

104. Do demons act through horoscopes, tarot cards, and other ways of seeing the future?

In principle, demons intervene only when they are invoked. Forms of guessing the future, such as horoscopes and tarot cards, do not call upon "hidden powers" or unknown spiritual beings; as such, they are not demonic. They are merely superstitious practices. But those who practice such superstitions open themselves up to the temptation to invoke such powers and unknown beings.

If, as we have said, it is impossible to know the future by invoking demons, then it is even less possible to do so using astrology, tarot cards, etc. The people who consult such superstitions are living proof that no benefit can be obtained through them. The only people who get any benefit from these deceits are the professional cheats and charlatans who practice them for money. They are skilled at measuring and generalizing their predictions so that they do not betray their falsehood.

105. What form do demons take when they appear to people?

As purely spiritual beings, demons do not have a determined visible form. As such, if they show themselves in a visible way, they can adopt any form they wish. Any human form, however beautiful, is within their power. They could appear as a known priest, as a confessor, or even as the Holy Father. Of course, the appearance of a demon is an extraordinary event—God does not ordinarily permit them to make themselves visible or to appear in any way they would choose. He only allows them to appear in a certain determined way to make it clear to us that it is actually a demon we are seeing.

Demons are permitted to appear as moving shadows, as monstrous freaks, or as very black, little men. The appearance of demons as little dark men appears repeatedly in Christian literature, starting with the Desert Fathers and continuing up to the writings of St. Teresa of Avila and St. Thérèse of Lisieux (in one of her dreams).

When the Bible speaks of Satan as a serpent (Genesis 3) or a dragon (Revelation 12), it is saying that he has the fierce, monstrous, poisonous, and astute character of these beings. In no way, though, does the devil truly look like a dragon or serpent; he continues to be a beautiful angel by nature, even though he is completely repugnant morally. He has suffered deformation only in his person, not in his nature. Given that these two things are inseparable, he really is a monster, a deformed being, someone that causes repugnance and aversion.

106. Can a demon cause a false vision in a mystic?

Though angels and demons have the power to infuse visions and locutions in human minds, God rarely permits them to do so. We can see that such visions and locutions would produce great confusion in souls. So God allows them only on very rare occasions and when the person has the means to discover the truth. Of course, if it were not for the Most High restraining the power of demons, they would regularly appear as angels or saints. There have even been reported cases in which a demon has taken the appearance of Our Lord Himself.

In the truly exceptional case of a mystical revelation to a soul, of which a spiritual director has his doubts about the demon concerned, there are two criteria that can be followed:

1. Follow all inspirations that bring one to good as if they come from God.

2. Obey one's spiritual director above any private revelation.

If a vision, apparition, or locution causes us to do good—that is, incites us to works of charity, prayer, and sacrifice—we should follow it as if it came directly from God. With this rule of conduct, all scruples will be wiped away and one avoids wasting time trying to look for the origin of the inspirations of the soul.

Now then, the direction of one's confessor or spiritual director must be followed before the message of any supposed private revelation. It does not matter how good or noble the revelation may be; all things must be subordinated to obedience to one's confessor. If the revelation comes from a demon, one of two things will occur: it will be in conflict with the direction of one's confessor, or it will soon stop leading one to good and begin inciting one toward evil. But if the revelation truly is from God, there will be no conflict between the revelation and the direction of one's spiritual director because obedience to the spiritual director is obedience to God.

We should always remember the maxim, "Obey always as long as it is not a sin." Even mystics are not free from obedience to spiritual direction; they should never trust their own judgment as to the authenticity of a vision or locution. In fact, a mystic is *more* subject to obedience because of the danger of falling into pride. If he is not careful, what happened to the devil can happen to him— pride can corrupt the gift he has received.

I have a special knowledge of this matter because, many years ago, I was chosen to be the spiritual director of a soul who was granted some extraordinary gifts. There was no doubt as to the veracity of these gifts, as I put them to the test on several occasions. But little by little, this person began not to heed my counsels. He thought himself to be so advanced in perfection that he could be guided directly by the Holy Spirit. Upon seeing that a terrible pride was appearing on the horizon, my counsels became orders. But the person chose to follow his own inspirations more than what I said. Gradually over the next few years, I could see that he was becoming more and more proud. Finally, I gave him an ultimatum: obey my direction or I would no longer be his spiritual director. In the end, he chose his own way, which, according to him, was that of the Holy Spirit. A year later, I found out from friends that he had fallen into a life of grave sin and had lost all the spiritual gifts I had witnessed. This terrible story serves as a reminder that, on the road to holiness, there are many who choose to remain in the gutter and whose names we will never know.

107. Can a demon cause the stigmata?

Yes, a demon can cause the *stigmata*, which are the wounds Christ suffered during His passion and death. In the past,

I did not believe this was possible because I considered the stigmata to be a phenomenon indicating divine approval of the person who bears them. Other mystical phenomena are hidden and are given for the good of the one who possesses them, whereas the stigmata are essentially given for the benefit of others. That is why they are external marks and are, as I once believed, a type of divine confirmation of the person's holiness. As St. Paul teaches, "Let no man trouble me; for I bear on my body the marks of Jesus" (Gal 6:17). If St. Paul is speaking here of the stigmata, then it would seem to corroborate the idea that a stigmatic has God's favor (which is the typical impression among people who know of the phenomenon). Nonetheless, later in my life, I learned of a "pseudo-messiah" who appeared to have bleeding wounds on certain parts of his body. Though these wounds were not the stigmata per se, his skin still bled.

So what conclusion can we draw from all this? Maybe the great lesson we can learn from such an anecdotal story is that the same God who gives us the signs to know the truth has also given us the intelligence to discern these signs. The God of the intellect has delighted Himself in giving us these types of enigmas for us to work them out.

In any case, the origin of a case of the stigmata, as in any another mystical phenomenon, will be deduced by the fruits that are produced in the life of this person. "By their fruits you will know them" (Mt 7:16). The fruits of the Evil One are pride and disobedience—in conclusion, sin. The fruits of a soul of God are humility, obedience, and a life of sacrifice and virtue. I repeat again that the fact that the stigmata can be caused by a demon is something anecdotal and accidental, but the lesson that can be learned from it is very important for any ecclesiastical field: everything can be faked except virtue. Signs, theological reasoning, intentions, etc., are all susceptible to being twisted and manipulated. The only thing that cannot be simulated is virtue.

108. Is the Antichrist the devil?

No. Many people, including some clergymen, erroneously identify the biblical figure of the Antichrist with the devil. In the Bible, the Antichrist is always presented as a human being. Revelation 13:18 expressly states that "666," the number of the Antichrist, is the "number of a man." Therefore, the Antichrist is not a demon but rather a man who propagates hate, war, and evil. Infamous historical figures such as Nero, Napoleon, and especially Hitler are types of the Antichrist.

The very name *anti-Christ* also tells us much about this nefarious figure. We are dealing with a person who works contrary to Christ. He is Christ's *opposite*. Jesus Christ spreads love, peace, and mercy; the Antichrist will spread hate, war, and vengeance. One is a humble figure who ended up being crucified; the other is a proud and triumphalistic figure. One has a father who is God; the other has Satan as his spiritual father. Both are "wonder-workers"; both have followers.

As an aside, hundreds of people have asked me what the significance of the number 666 is and to whom it corresponds. I always tell them that when the end times come, its meaning will be understood. It is a coded message to help us recognise the Antichrist, and until the moment arrives, there is no sense in making speculations. This prophecy is similar to the Old Testament prophecies about the coming of the Messiah. They were not fully comprehensible before their fulfillment, but their meaning was perfectly clear after the events occurred. The number 666 is a sign by which we can recognise the Antichrist so that, when he comes, the meaning of the prophecy will be clear.

109. What does St. Paul mean when he says that Christ will bring the demons in his triumphal court?

> [Jesus] disarmed the principalities and powers and made a public example of them, triumphing over them in him. (Col 2:15)

When St. Paul here speaks of "principalities and powers," he is referring to the angels belonging to those two hierarchies which rebelled. Some angelic principalities and powers remained faithful, while others became demoniac by their rebellion. What will the rebels be disarmed of? Of their power over humanity. Demons exercise real power over humanity due to sin. This influence is exercised through temptation and is ultimately destroyed by the Cross of Christ. This disarming of the principalities and powers is a liberation, just like that of God's chosen people from Egypt, who escaped the yoke of slavery.

When St. Paul says that Christ has led them away in triumph, he is thinking about the image of the victorious generals entering into the metropolis followed on foot by the captured enemy leaders. This literary image conveys that there was a real fight between the Messiah and

Satan—a spiritual fight, but a true and authentic fight nonetheless.

Jesus' triumphal court is not like those of worldly courts. Spirits do not occupy space nor can they line up. Rather the public exhibition of which St. Paul speaks is the exposition before all the angels and blessed of each of the victories that Jesus achieved in His battles against the evil spirits.

110. How can I tell if a particular thought or desire is from the devil?

As St. John in his first letter tells us: "Beloved, do not believe every spirit, but test the spirits to see whether they are of God: for many false prophets have gone out into the world" (1 Jn 4:1).

St. Ignatius of Loyola, in his profound *Spiritual Exercises*, offers several rules for the discernment of spirits. These rules serve to illuminate the manner in which a demon acts when tempting a soul, and an understanding of such rules can help us discern whether a particular desire is from the Evil One.

In his first rule, St. Ignatius notes that in people who go from mortal sin to mortal sin, the devil commonly proposes to them apparent pleasures, seeking to keep them bound in sensual delights and pleasures so that they might grow in their sins and vices.

The second rule pertains to people who are going about an intense purification of their sins and vices so that they might serve God more faithfully. Here, the devil—contrary to the first rule—seeks to sadden and frustrate their progress by putting up obstacles and disquieting them with false fears, so that they might give up the practice of virtue.

In his twelfth rule, St. Ignatius likens the devil to a commander of an army bent on conquering, examining an enemy's strengths and weaknesses, and attacking at the weakest point. As the enemy of human nature, the devil looks at our virtues and attacks us in the area where we are weakest and which is most critical to our eternal salvation.

Thus, if we understand and apply these rules to a particular thought or desire, we can more easily discern whether a particular inspiration is from the Evil One.

INDEX

Acknowledgments

Sincere thanks to Bishop Samuel Aquila for his eloquent words in the foreword; the priests who reviewed the manuscript and offered many helpful suggestions: Fr. John Horn, Fr. John Michet, and Fr. Richard Fineo; Devin Schadt for his striking cover design; Matthew Pinto and the staff of Ascension Press for their efforts in bringing this book to print; and most especially, to Our Lady, the Blessed Virgin Mary, the true "Morning Star" and powerful protector against the forces of darkness.

About the Author

Fr. José Antonio Fortea is a priest of the Diocese of Alcalá de Henares (Madrid) in Spain and an expert in the field of demonology. An approved exorcist of his diocese, he has conducted numerous exorcisms and lectures on this topic throughout the world. In 1998, he successfully defended his thesis for a licentiate degree in theology, entitled "Exorcism in the Present Age," under the direction of the secretary of the Commission for the Doctrine of the Faith of the Spanish Bishops Conference.